Give My Kind Regards to the Ladies

THE LIFE OF
LITTLETON QUINTON
WASHINGTON

David Scott Turk

HERITAGE BOOKS
2011

HERITAGE BOOKS
AN IMPRINT OF HERITAGE BOOKS, INC.

Books, CDs, and more—Worldwide

For our listing of thousands of titles see our website
at
www.HeritageBooks.com

Published 2011 by
HERITAGE BOOKS, INC.
Publishing Division
100 Railroad Ave. #104
Westminster, Maryland 21157

Copyright © 2001 David Scott Turk

Other Heritage Books by the author:
A Family's Path in America: The Lees and Their Continuing Legacy
Give My Kind Regards to the Ladies: The Life of Littleton Quinton Washington
The Memorialists: An Antebellum History of Alleghany, Craig, and Monroe Counties of Western Virginia, 1812-60
The Union Hole: Unionist Activity and Local Conflict in Western Virginia

All rights reserved. No part of this book may be reproduced or transmitted in any form or by any means, electronic or mechanical, including photocopying, recording or by any information storage and retrieval system without written permission from the author, except for the inclusion of brief quotations in a review.

International Standard Book Numbers
Paperbound: 978-0-7884-1806-8
Clothbound: 978-0-7884-8889-4

Table of Contents

His Father's Son	1
The Rise of an Insider	14
"Grateful for the Offer"	34
View of Reconstruction from a Southern Correspondent	65
Editorial Wars, Greenbacks, and Redemption	89
"You Owe Him Nothing"	122
Vestige of a Legacy	138
Genealogical Charts	150
Bibliography	152
Index	164

Acknowledgments

This book was made possible by many people who offered me time, knowledge, and character. My wife Janet and son Ryan were critical in all three departments. My father, Howard S. Turk, an author in his own right, provided me with the will to keep trying. My stepmother Karen Ray also offered much encouragement. My mother, Ann Turk, provided me with equal appreciation as well as grounding knowledge of her heritage, which has kept me writing all these years. My brother-in-law Glenn Vogel kept me sane in an insane world, and so did my many friends: Sunil Setia; Nick Prevas; Greg Blank & family; The Wagner & Welty families; my cousins Tim Bisson and Rob Yarborough; Larry Mogavero; Barbara Harman; Anthony Corbitt, who actually asks for me to autograph my work for him; Mark Kline, the backgammon specialist; Kevin O'Hare, the New England lawyer; the trench-warfare loving Jim Herzog; Bill Licotovich, Tom Connor, Assistant Directors Larry Cooper and Robert J. Finan II; my supervisor Debra Jenkins; and countless others. I especially thank my friend W. Carlyle Turner, who regularly reminds me that I do have a sense of humor somewhere. It is he who deserves much for his constant cheer through my numerous trials.

Academic thanks are in order for encouragement by Professors Jane Turner Censer and Peter Henriques of George Mason University; Professors James Millar and Donald Crowl of Longwood College; Frederick S. Calhoun for fine-tuning my research skills; John White and the staff at the Southern Historical Collection at the University of North Carolina at Chapel Hill; the staff at the University of Virginia Special Collections; Duke University Special Collections; Tulane

University Special Collections; the National Archives; the Manuscripts Room at the Library of Congress; and the Virginia Historical Society. I thank Bob Hufty for his knowledge of the family. I also thank Julie Campbell, Editor of *Virginia Cavalcade* at the Virginia State Library for her early faith in my work. Thanks also to Kate Ives for making sense of this manuscript. Most of all I give my regards to the ladies, particularly the southern belle, to whom I dedicate this work.

A Father's Son

He was a newsman, a lobbyist, a servant for two totally distinct governments, political enthusiast, cynic, and presidential relation. Littleton Quinton Dennis Washington (1825-1902) was a man literally lost in shadows. He was born with George Washington's family name. Although he grew up in prestige, he was not wealthy. He loved politics, and grew up a few blocks from the Capitol. Washington attached himself to a powerful politician, Speaker of the House Robert Mercer Taliaferro Hunter. As Washington matured, he grew as a political protégé to Hunter. He followed Hunter out of the Union in 1861, and engaged himself in the Confederate States Government in the capacity of Chief Clerk of the State Department. At a critical point in his life, he was the knowledgeable second to Confederate Secretary of State Judah Benjamin. Indeed, Washington knew much of the War's last months, including the Confederacy's early peace initiatives and Lincoln's assassination. After the war, Washington returned to the capital city and suffered in postwar times as a poorly paid newsman. In an unpaid capacity, he served as a lobbyist for the Democratic Party in the South. He maintained old ties to ex-Confederates through the periods of Reconstruction and Readjustment, writing many letters to his cohorts. Although pardoned and a news correspondent until his death, Washington was a forgotten man. Even in history, Washington was a shadow. His name was constantly misquoted in all ways. The most likely reason was the fact that his name was nearly the same initials as Confederate statesman L.Q.C. Lamar. Many incorrectly assumed it was the same, and call him Lucius Quintius Washington.

Even the existing record of his life confirmed Washington as a

A Father's Son

shadowy figure. With a few noted exceptions, the history of his life was based on Washington's own letters and that of the surviving documentation of others who responded. He was a proliferate correspondent with figures of the day such as Robert M.T. Hunter, Colonel Lewis Harvie of Amelia County, and Frank Gildart Ruffin. His social circles were wide. Contacts and friends included Henry Wise, James A. Seddon, Judah Benjamin, William W. Corcoran, and many Washington D.C. figures of the 1870s and 1880s. It was possible to reconstruct the framework of Washington's life through this correspondence and cross-references with public records at the National Archives and Library of Congress.

As an observer of American history as it happened, L.Q. Washington crossed bridges. His father was a federal officeholder from the earliest days of the nation, and he grew up in antebellum Washington D.C. After serving in several positions during the fiery days of the Confederacy, Washington worked as an unofficial booster for the South in the Reconstruction, working for the readmission of Virginia to the Union. By his death in 1902, Washington was the one of the grand old men of the Confederacy. Yet he was completely forgotten in many circles. As he lived in an environment unfriendly to ex-Confederates, and among the hordes of young correspondents working near Congress, Washington's postwar success in the business world was limited. Because of his voluminous correspondence, L.Q. Washington stands out as a figure who described politics in a particularly Southern view and nothing remains hidden: disgust, jealousy, joys, all are here. It would not be in Washington's

A Father's Son

character to restrain himself when addressing his intended readership.

L.Q. Washington's interest in genealogy and journalism was a trait passed on from his detail-oriented father, Lund Washington. In the painstaking detail which his son adopted, the father detailed his proud genealogy.

> In the year 1832 I was in King George, at Woodstock my birthplace-I was at Townshend Dades (who married one of the Daughters of Rev'd Wm Stuart) he informed me that Albion was the Seat of the of the Townshend Family and that he had found the Tombstone of the late Robert Townsend...[1]

Lund Washington wrote these words around the year 1846. He detailed family accounts that were bound to be lost otherwise. Aware of the pride of the Washington name and all the responsibility that came with it, he meticulously noted all genealogical connections with precision. From it, the complex personality of the man was explained. In 1846, Lund Washington was an older gentleman in his second marriage. He was the namesake of his paternal uncle, who was entrusted with the stewardship of Mount Vernon while General George Washington was at war against the British. His father, Robert Washington, was a distant cousin of the future President. The younger Lund was a young man during the Revolutionary War, having been born in 1767. Unlike his famous cousin, he stayed at the family estate in King George County. Lund grew up in the

---

[1] Unpublished genealogy, ca 1846, by Lund Washington, Papers of the Washington Family, Manuscript Division, Library of Congress.

A Father's Son

tidewater countryside of Virginia, learning from his family those important connective details he later wrote down.[2]

> I have seen a Deed executed in 1650 by Lord Berkeley to Francis Townsend for 2200 acres of land on Chotank Creek on the Potomac-which is the same land the descendents of the Townsend family lived on and where (at Albion) the two Washingtons John& Lawrence first settled.[3]

Lund's marital lineage was equally as interesting as his own. He married into two prominent first Virginia families when he married Susannah Monroe Grayson in 1793. His marriage linked him to a signer of the Declaration of Independence, William Grayson, and a future President of the United States, James Monroe. The marriage produced eleven children, the last born in October 1812.[4]

Sadly, there remains little detail of Lund Washington's domestic life with the exception of his occupation. Lund remained in King George County until 1786, when he moved to the thriving of Alexandria. He was apprenticed to Colonel R.T. Hooe and learned the merchant trade. When his cousin George Washington became President of the United States, his prospects improved. Patronage was a reality in the early days of the

---

[2]Ibid.
[3]Ibid. Lund's father Robert was John Washington's second son.
[4]Edward S. Lewis, "Ancestry of James Monroe," *William and Mary College Quarterly*, Vol. 3, Series 2, 1923, 174; Unpublished Genealogy, Library of Congress. Lewis was a descendant of the Washingtons and chronicled much history on the family from his home in St. Louis.

A Father's Son

national government. President Washington appointed two postmasters of the developing capital city of the fledgling United States during the first seven years of his term. There is no post office building, so the postmaster maintained his office within his residence. Lund, with a young wife and children, was the third person picked by his cousin to this appointment. The likelihood of reasoning was simple: Lund was young, trustworthy, and sturdy. The new capital city was built on a swamp, and the previous two postmasters, Mr. Johnson and Mr. Richmond, died in office, Richmond within five months of his appointment. After such losses, thirty-two year old Lund Washington made a feasible choice. His appointment was dated May 26, 1796.[5]

Lund settled into his residence on the north side of East Capitol Street, near First Street, Northwest. Consequently, the post office moved twelve blocks, since Mr. Richmond had lived at 13th and F Streets. Lund worked in this position until the end of President Washington's term. Deciding to remain in the city, Lund knew he needed to find some occupation outside the realm of patronage. Rejecting the merchant trade, Lund took advantage of his shorthand and writing skills. Location and writing prowess made him an ideal candidate for a Congressional correspondent. Lund had increased his sources, making important political connections during the two years of his position as postmaster.

---

[5] "Descendants of Two John Washingtons," *The Virginia Magazine of History and Biography*, Vol. XXVI, 1918, 417; Wilhelmus Bogart Bryan, *A History of the National Capital From Its Foundation Through the Period of the Adoption of the Organic Act, Vol. I, 1790-1814* (New York, NY: The Macmillan Company, 1914), 263.

A Father's Son

The dual occupations of politics and news reporting affected Lund and his family for generations.[6]

The newspaper industry was new to Washington, D.C. Correspondents flooded the town from far-off cities such as Boston and Charleston. Joseph Gales, Jr., and William W. Seaton started the District of Columbia-based *National Intelligencer* purely on the strength of the well-publicized fights between Alexander Hamilton Federalists and Thomas Jefferson Democrat-Republicans. Undoubtedly Lund had a strong connection to this publication. Along with the success of his work as correspondent, Lund involved himself in the promotion of civil works in a significant situation. In 1814, the year the British burned Washington D.C., Lund was active with newspaper notables such as Gales, Seaton, and Mayor John Peter Van Ness to fund a new church in the city's first and second wards. By late 1815, funds were secured and St. John's Church was built near present day Lafayette Square.[7]

Prosperity continued for Lund's family into the Monroe

---

[6] "Descendants," *Virginia Magazine*, XXVI, 417; Bryan, *A History*, 263; Fred A. Emery, "Washington Newspaper Correspondents," *Records of the Columbia Historical Society of Washington, D.C.*, Volume 35-36 (Washington, D.C.: Columbia Historical Society, 1935), 254; Lewis, "Ancestry of Monroe," *William and Mary Quarterly*, 174.

[7] Emery, "Washington Newspaper Correspondents," *Records of the Columbia Historical Society*, Washington, D.C., 254; Hon. Alexander B. Hagner, "History and Reminiscences of St. John's Church, Washington, D.C.," *Records of the Columbia Historical Society* Washington D.C. Volume 12 (Washington, D.C.: Columbia Historical Society, 1909), 90.

Administration. By 1811, Lund owned two lots on Union and 4 1/2 Streets. One of his eldest sons, William T. Washington, worked as a clerk in the office of Secretary of War John C. Calhoun from September, 1817. Although this was a temporary appointment due to the fact that he was still a minor, William worked at the War Department until he left for West Point as a cadet in April 1818. Son Peter G. Washington was prosperous in practicing law. Another son, Lund, was mentioned in later records. However, Lund's own personal life during this period was difficult. After a marriage of almost thirty years, Susannah Washington died at the age of fifty-three on April 20, 1822.[8]

A year after his wife's death, Lund traveled to the eastern shore of Maryland, to Johnson's Bay. By this body of water was the historic town of Snow Hill. By Lund's own account, the Johnsons were a successful family of planters who resided in the area for many generations. Lund's interest in Snow Hill was to visit one of General George Washington's officers during the American Revolution, Colonel Leven Handy. The Handy family was well acquainted with John and Susanna Johnson, and through this contact Lund Washington met their daughter Sally. The aged Washington took an extended stay at Snow Hill. He wrote that

---

[8]Lund Washington, Edward A. Lewis, Edward S. Lewis II, and Edward McE. Lewis, comp. *Pedigrees of Lewis and Kindred Lines*, unpublished manuscript, Missouri Historical Society of St. Louis, Missouri, 1927, 301W; Petition of Lund Washington, March 29, 1844, to accompany H.R. No. 280, Report No. 382, 28th Congress, 1st Session. National Archives; Genealogy of Lund Washington, Washington Family Papers, Manuscript Division, Library of Congress.

A Father's Son

after six weeks-- "about three weeks before my marriage-I thought that Miss Johnson would suit me..but determined to keep the matter a secret until I was ready for its consummation..."⁹

The secret marriage took place on April 11, 1823. The manner of subsequent events Lund recorded carefully.

> ...I believed she had the nobility of Virtue-on the evening before our marriage-I popped the question, she consented-and I insisted on being married the next day at 12 Oclock-she consented -and the next day in the presence of my friend Henry Burdick and his wife I was married by John Chalmers a Methodist Minister and two other married Ladies.¹⁰

The marriage caused problems within the Washington family, as many of them disapproved of Lund's action. His children reacted strongly, perhaps due to the bride's young age. Lund himself appeared puzzled by their behavior.

> The news flew rapidly about the city and raised a foolish hubbub of slander and falsehood, my daughters Susan and Betsey were invited to spend the evening at the House where my wife was staying-and in a few minutes after their arrival Betsey began to reproach Mrs. Peggy Crossfield with keeping my marriage a Secret -And my Son Lund prevented Mr Rind of Geo[rge]town from publishing my marriage in the newspaper.¹¹

---

[9] Unpublished Memoirs, Lund Washington, Washington Family Papers, Manuscript Division, Library of Congress.
[10] Ibid.
[11] Ibid.

A Father's Son

In this atmosphere, Lund began his second marriage. The couple wanted to start a family immediately. A son, Emory Peyton Washington, was born on July 29, 1824, but died three weeks later. Further tragedy occurred when a pregnant Sally Washington traveled to Snow Hill in the late summer of 1825. Upon arrival she received the news that both her parents had died. However, hardship turned to joy on November 3, 1825. Littleton Dennis Quinton Washington, a healthy boy, was born.[12]

Lund continued to work as a Congressional correspondent and moved his young family into a house on B Street, between 2nd and 3rd Streets. On the same block was John G. Robinson, a carpenter; Thomas Donn, a coach maker; and Thomas Bowen, a local tailor. Washington's second family continued to grow. Sally gave birth to a daughter, Mary Mason Washington, on October 27, 1827. However, Littleton and Mary were to be the only surviving children of this union; the remaining children, Susan Quinton (1830), George Johnson Washington (1834), and Esther Matilda Washington (1836) died as infants.[13]

Sometime during this period of loss, Lund began work at the Comptroller of the Currency office within the Treasury Department. His annual salary started at $1,400 a year. It was

---

[12] Ibid.
[13] Washington Topham, "First Railroad Into Washington and Its Three Depots," *Records of the Columbia Historical Society of Washington, D.C., Volume 27* (Washington, D.C.: Columbia Historical Society, 1925), 186; Lund Washington unpublished memoirs, Washington Family Papers, Manuscript Division, Library of Congress.

A Father's Son

Lund's wish to educate his two young children in the best schools possible. So in 1841, at the ages of sixteen and fourteen, Littleton and Mary were sent to Carlisle, Pennsylvania. Littleton attended classes at Dickinson College. However, after a short time, their return was forced by the cutback of Lund's salary from $1,400 to $1,000 per year. Littleton remembered the income cut into adulthood, and money became an obsessive issue with Lund as he reached old age. The sudden shifts in fortune haunted him. In March 1844, he claimed that his son William, who had passed away, had not been reimbursed for his early work with Calhoun in 1818. A grant of $200 was made in June 1844.[14]

At the end of April 1845 Lund, aged seventy-eight, resigned from the position of clerk in the office of the First Comptroller of the Treasury. He formally issued his resignation to Treasury Secretary Robert Walker on April 25th. The fear of losing money was a legacy never lost on his son, who was every bit his father's boy.[15]

The twenty-four year old Littleton, known as "L.Q." or "L.Q.W." in correspondence, showed a great interest in his father's genealogical work. Gathering all the family stories he could, Littleton eagerly wrote them down. One of these stories, dated December 10, 1849, was as follows:

---

[14]Ibid.; Memorial of Lund Washington, accompanied by H.R. No. 280, March 29, 1844, 28th Congress, 1st Session, National Archives; Committee of Claims, Twenty-Eighth Congress, Session I, 925, National Archives.

[15]R.T. Walker to Lund Washington, April 25, 1845, Box 2, Washington Family Papers, Manuscript Division, Library of Congress.

A Father's Son

> My father Lund Washington told me yesterday this anecdote, derived from by him from his uncle, Lund W, who was manager of Genl W's estates-A man named Adams in Alexa[ndria] had obtained flour from the Genls mill to the value of L500. During the war he tendered payment to Lund W-in continental money, which was then greatly depreciated. It was very naturally refused, on the ground that L500 in contl money was no payt of a debt of that amount. An account of the affair was sent to the General who wrote back- "I cannot do any act which will damn the credit of my country-You must take the money"[16]

L.Q. began translating his father's genealogical material, much of which was written in the 1840's. He was keenly aware of the connection to the President. Not unlike George Washington, L.Q. emulated the role of a young man on the make and was ever indulgent in his family's genteel lifestyle. Part of that lifestyle included seasonal visits to the healing waters of the Virginia springs. In the early 1850's, the Washingtons made numerous trips to White Sulphur Springs in Virginia's Allegheny Mountains or Warrenton's Sulphur Springs. Clusters of houses, or rows, drew famous statesman and rich merchants. There was lavish dining, dancing, and sport. The hot Washington summer drove the elderly Lund to Warrenton in July 1852, while L.Q. was at the White Sulphur Springs, a place he frequented

---

[16]Notes by Littleton Dennis Quinton Washington, December 10, 1849 in Box 2, Washington Family Papers, Manuscript Division, Library of Congress. From this point, Littleton Dennis Quinton Washington will be denoted as L.Q. or Washington.

A Father's Son

throughout his life.[17] This was detailed in a letter Lund wrote to his son:

> I left the City yesterday and arrived here in the evening-I arrived at the rail Road at Alexa at 12 Minutes after 9 and in 3 Minutes was in progress like lightning the road went South West for 30 Miles and then the cars took the Menasses Gap Road and we took the Stage-the road was to the West, and quite bad we arrived at Warrenton at 2 oClock Dined and at 3 Oclock were on the road to the Springs-the Road for 2 Miles was to the West and the remaining four to the South West...[18]

The letter continued with references to the family and his own failing health.

> Peter promises to be here next week-This is a delightful place, far superior to any thing I had anticipated-I had not heard from you since your first letter up to the time of starting...The Springs being East of the Blue Ridge; the climate is the same as it is in, the City, but the air is more refreshing. I advise you to come to this place as soon as you can, and you will have good Sulphur Water to drink, good fare, and you can take good care of my home-the fare here is excellent and the Price is 9 Dollars per Week--Your Mother, and Mary and Peter and all friends in the City were well-I was much fatigued yesterday-today I am better.[19]

---

[17]Ibid.; Lund Washington to L.Q. Washington, July 31, 1852, Box 2, Washington Family Papers, Manuscript Division, Library of Congress.
[18]Ibid.
[19]Ibid.

A Father's Son

Lund's details in the letter revealed his deep love of family and an ever-present mind set on cost effectiveness. The tone was one of complete trust and respect. However, Lund was not physically healthy.

The sense of mortality Lund Washington felt in this letter was justified. In 1853, at the age of 86, he died at his home and was buried in the city's Congressional Cemetery. His was a useful and energetic life. L.Q. patterned his life to be every bit the same.[20]

---

[20]Lewis, "Ancestry of James Monroe," *William & Mary Quarterly*, 3, 2, 173-174.

The Rise of an Insider

The mid 1850s was an adventurous time for L.Q. Washington. He found a government position on the West Coast during the later Gold Rush days, followed by a stint as a campaign advisor for a candidate to the nation's highest office. A rise in political fortunes was certain. He enjoyed the benefits of his rise as an insider, a man behind the scenes. Power and influence were evident in his early efforts, but most importantly, they assisted him in later labors.

L.Q. Washington made his way into the political world of the 1850s. In October 1853, he owned shares in the Washington Library Company, an early subscription facility prevalent among the city elite. As his father had done, Washington rose in personal esteem by investing in the community. Largely thanks to his family's good reputation, L.Q. began the 1850s working for the Treasury Department. President Franklin Pierce's Secretary of the Treasury, James Murray Mason, appointed L.Q. to the office of Deputy Collector of Customs in San Francisco, California on December 1, 1855.[1]

1855 San Francisco was a boomtown. By this time it had passed the more prosperous days of the Gold Rush, which started near the center of the state in 1848. San Francisco changed from a sleepy and strategic coastal holding to a self-contained city. This was the environment in which L.Q. arrived.

---

[1] Washington Library Certificate of Stock, October 13, 1853, Washington Family Papers, Container 2, Library of Congress; James M. Mason to Milton S. Latham Esqr, January 1, 1856, No. 663, RG 36, Records of the Department of the Collector of Customs, National Archives.

The Rise of an Insider

L.Q.'s duties as Deputy Collector primarily involved in securing tax revenues. However, it was not easy work. L.Q. wrote a few letters to his half-brother Peter. In September 1856 he noted the unruly nature of life in San Francisco. Worried over personal protection, L.Q. wrote that "neither the Commander of the Army or Navy here care anything about the preservation of order...We have at the Presidio (some 4 miles off) 30 soldiers & it would take a week to get 500 men..."[2]

L.Q. received his first taste of politics in San Francisco. He befriended Judge Matthew Hall McAllister and several others who took an early interest in local Democratic politics. He proudly wrote Peter Washington,

> ...We have here a Young Men's Dem. Club so organized as to exclude all vigilant sympathisers ...I send you our resolutions, the first two of which I penned. We number 3000 members already-- double all the other clubs combined & carried the late primary elections here in almost every ward.[3]

Customs controlled all commerce to and from the port and trade facilities of the town, which had been large since ships arrived regularly. However, L.Q. researched various areas of commerce trade law, including past cases. He invested long hours to ensure careful application of trade law. In February

---

[2] L.Q. Washington to Peter G. Washington, September 4, 1856, Papers of Peter Grayson Washington (MSS 2769), Special Collections Department, University of Virginia Library.
[3] Ibid.

The Rise of an Insider

1857, he wrote his supervisor, Milton S. Latham:

> By reference to page 6 of General Regulations of the Department no. 65, you will find a reference to a decision of the Supreme Court Jan. Term 1846 in the case of McKean Buchanan vs. James Alexander to this effect, to wit; That monies in the hands of a disbursing officer of the Govt cannot be reached by processes of attachment. Such attempts to garnishee are therefore to be resisted.[4]

L.Q.'s position was subject to political appointment. About the time that saw the election of President James Buchanan, he took a leave of absence to travel home. Secretary Mason approved the leave without the loss of pay, allowing him one month's time.[5] The actual reason for his journey was partially politically motivated. He wrote Peter Washington that "a number of office seekers will go on from here & I may be struck down without an opportunity to defend myself."[6] Latham was interested in retaining his services if elected a California Congressman. L.Q. arrived in Washington about February 15th, with instructions to leave Washington for San Francisco on

---

[4] L.Q. Washington to Hon. Milton S. Latham, February 17, 1857, Records of the Collector of Customs, San Francisco, Letter Book, 116, National Archives.

[5] Mason to Latham, February 17, 1857, No. 853 in Letterbook, RG36, Records of the Collector of Customs, San Francisco, National Archives.

[6] L.Q. Washington to Peter G. Washington, January 4, 1857, Papers of Peter Grayson Washington (MSS 2769), Special Collections Department, University of Virginia Library.

The Rise of an Insider

March 20, 1857, when the leave officially ended.[7]

During L.Q.'s leave of absence, President Pierce's term ended. President James Buchanan's administration brought new faces to California, changing the political landscape and making L.Q.'s position uncertain. Most notable was Latham's replacement as San Francisco's collector by Benjamin Franklin Washington. The latter Washington was a native of Jefferson County, West Virginia, and a descendant of George Washington's brother Lawrence. L.Q. was reappointed as Deputy Collector on July 29, 1857, at the salary of $3,600 per annum. Another Washington, a namesake named George, was appointed Cashier at $3,000 per annum; the Buchanan appointments appeared an invasion of the Washington family. However, all was not well between family members. Within a month, Collector Benjamin Washington sent L.Q. notice that he intended to replace him.[8]

> It is my intention on the 1st of September, proximo, to appoint John H. Wise, Deputy, in the place now held by yourself. It would be gratifying to me, should

---

[7]Ibid.; Mason to Latham, February 19, 1857, No. 853 in Letterbook, RG 36, Collector of Customs, National Archives.

[8]Secretary of the Treasury Howell Cobb to Benjamin F. Washington, July 29, 1857 (No. 1) in Letterbook, RG 36, Records of the Collector of Customs, National Archives; Jefferson County Historical Society, *The Washington Homes of Jefferson County, West Virginia* (Charlestown, WV: Jefferson County Historical Society, 1988), 9-10; Benjamin F. Washington to L.Q. Washington, August 24, 1857, Washington Family Papers, Manuscripts Division, Library of Congress.

it meet your views, if you would send me your resignation.[9]

The irony was that his replacement, John H. Wise, was a relative of the popular Governor of Virginia, Henry Alexander Wise. The elder Wise and L.Q. would cross paths again in a short time.

With a replacement in his stead as Deputy Collector in San Francisco, L.Q. returned to the Nation's Capital. While he toiled with an uncertain future during the next year, he stayed in touch with politically-minded Virginians. Southern firebrand Edmund Ruffin noted L.Q., and a man named Boulware met him in the public room of the National Hotel on January 16, 1859. Always astute in Southern politics, Ruffin remarked there was "a discussion on the policy of re-opening the African slave-trade-- B.[Boulware] against, & W. [Washington] and I stating the arguments in favor-"[10]

Ruffin and Washington saw each other frequently during this time, meeting one of several times in 1859. Late that year, John Brown and a band of men, both black and white, captured the arsenal near Harper's Ferry, Virginia. Brown led his men to Harper's Ferry and held the town's arsenal in a symbolic attack

---

[9]Benjamin F. Washington to L.Q. Washington, August 24, 1857, Washington Family Papers, Manuscripts Division, Library of Congress.
[10]Reprinted by permission of Louisiana State University Press from *The Diary of Edmund Ruffin, Volume I Toward Independence October, 1856-April, 1861*, edited by William Kauffman Scarborough, Entry of January 16, 1859, Copyright 1972 by Louisiana State University Press, 267. Boulware is probably William Boulware of Virginia.

The Rise of an Insider

on the institution of slavery. He held out until several of his men were killed by Virginia Militia. The South was angry and called for legislation to prevent a similar incident. Ruffin served in the House of Representatives in Washington, and met L.Q. shortly after the incident.

> ...Richmond papers of today containing reports of the sundry county meetings in reference to the abolition outbreak at Harper's Ferry, all of which passed strong resolutions. I hope that it is not all gas, which after effervescing & escaping will leave the body of the liquor flat, stale, & dead. Mr. Washington of this place, & Gen [Sydenham] Moore, M.C. of Alabama called & sat with me. Our conversation, as almost always of any southern men, on the present position of the north & the south.[11]

L.Q.'s ties to the Virginia delegation were strengthened when he started work for U.S. Senator Robert Mercer Taliaferro Hunter of Essex County, Virginia. By early 1860, L.Q. assisted Hunter with his political insight and "intelligence gathering" around the public rooms of the capital city. He had begun work as a news correspondent shortly before, which aided him greatly. Hunter was a prospect for the Democratic presidential candidate in the election later that year, and L.Q. promoted Hunter for several key reasons. From his perspective, a Virginian in the White House

---

[11] Reprinted by permission of Louisiana State University Press, Entry of December 10, 1859, in Scarborough, ed., *Diary of Edmund Ruffin, Volume I*, 378.

staved off war and promoted Southern measures. Hunter was known as a politician who reached across party lines and forged a plan for sectional peace. It probably didn't hurt that fellow Virginian Henry Alexander Wise was Hunter's opponent.[12]

The atmosphere around the choice of presidential candidates within the Democratic Party was tense. Northern Democrats favored Stephen A. Douglas of Illinois, while the Southern wing of the party favored Buchanan's Vice-President, John C. Breckinridge of Kentucky. Only moderates considered either Hunter or Wise. A test vote within the Virginia state party proved Hunter the clear winner in early 1860. Wise withdrew his name after the test vote. The divisive nature of the Democratic Party and Hunter's need for an active assistant lured L.Q. into the formal art of national campaign politics.[13]

The Democratic Party nominated their candidates at Charleston, South Carolina in April, 1860. There the ideological wings of the party clashed. The experience frustrated both Northern Democrats and moderates, who were essentially prevented from nominating a peace candidate. "Fire-eaters," or non-compromise Southern Democrats, led by Robert Yancey and others from deep Southern states, attempted to disrupt the

---

[12] John Eugene Fisher, *Statesman of the Lost Cause: R.M.T. Hunter and the Sectional Controversy, 1847-1887* (Ann Arbor, MI: UMI, 1968), dissertation, UVA, 192-193; Henry Harrison Simms, *The Life of Robert M.T. Hunter* (Richmond, VA: William Byrd Press, 1935), 140-141.
[13] Ibid., 142-143.

process. The attempt to "gag" or silence the moderates created consternation in moderate Virginia and other states. L.Q. cabled Hunter from the convention, "Improvement since yesterday Virginia and New York voted against the gag."[14]

By early May the sides were deadlocked. The "fire-eaters" walked out after their demand to immediately accept Breckinridge was not met. A motion was made to reconvene on June 18, 1860, in Baltimore, Maryland; However, the moderates desire to maintain the peace proved to be a block to convention continuance, and the lower Southern delegates would not attend. Stephen Douglas was the likely nominee, and any hope of a moderate candidate like Hunter was dashed. L.Q. knew this prior to Baltimore, and was understandably bitter. He held a special enmity for Louisiana politician John Slidell.[15]

> The fire-eaters were wrong in the programme...we could have nominated a man--most likely yourself. Indeed...we had a sure hand if they yielded to our line of policy..In my opinion he [Slidell] is the father of secession. His whole aim was...to break down Douglas and he would have killed you without a scrupple to get at Douglas.[16]

---

[14]Fisher, 192; Washington to Hunter, April 25, 1860, in Charles Henry Ambler, ed., *Annual Report of the American Historical Association for the Year 1916, Vol. II, Correspondence of Robert M.T. Hunter* (Washington, DC: American Historical Association, 1918), 320.
[15]Fisher, *Statesman*, 192.
[16]Ibid., 192-193., Washington to Hunter, May 5, 1860, Hunter-Garnett Family Papers (MSS 38-45), Special Collections

L.Q. intended to compile a record of the historic Charleston Convention, but other Virginia politicians, such as William Old, Jr., cautioned Hunter to forego any written opinion at that point.

> After leaving you I remembered a conversation I had with Mr. Washington in which I approved his intention to write out some reminiscences of the Charleston Convention. I have great confidence in his judgment, but our fight with Douglas, if one is necessary, requires most delicate management. It must be carried on as a state affair. The Virginia democracy must be the arbiters. Our course towards Douglas and his friends must be borne in mind, we built him up in Va, or *rather prevented his destruction.* We must wait for action by his friends before we commence hostilities in that State. Every feeling I have impels me to assail the man and his friends, but we must be careful in doing so. Can you present some such views to Mr. Washington?[17]

The Baltimore meeting went forward as predicted. Many Southern voters never showed up. Douglas was nominated as the Democratic candidate, and Hunter received marginal votes. L.Q. felt the Baltimore Convention could have helped Hunter only if some of the missing Southern voters had attended.[18]

With the campaign over, L.Q. withdrew to the White Sulphur Springs in August. There he met up with other prominent

---

Department, University of Virginia Library.
[17]William Old, Jr. to R.M.T. Hunter, May 11, 1860, in Ambler, ed., *Annual Report*, 325.
[18]Emerson David Fite, *The Political Campaign of 1860* (New York: The Macmillan Company, 1911), 107-108; Fisher, *Statesman*, 193.

The Rise of an Insider

Southerners in need of recuperation from the campaign. Edmund Ruffin was there, and noted the company.

> Senator [James] Chesnut of S.C., & Judge Perkins of La., P[atrick] H[enry] Aylett, Judge [Thomas S.] Gholson, Daniel London of Va, Gov [William] McWillie of Miss. among the visitors. Also L.Q. Washington of D.C. one of the most agreeable & well-informed.[19]

According to Ruffin, the bitter talk of secession arose. It was contingent on whether the Republican Party candidate, Abraham Lincoln, was elected in November.[20]

Although L.Q. temporarily detached from active politics, he observed the unfolding events with interest. He remained at White Sulphur until about August 28th, when Ruffin again noted L.Q.'s presence there in his diary. Upon returning to Washington, D.C., events quickly unfolded. Several months later the election of Abraham Lincoln, followed by the standoff to resupply provisions at Fort Sumter, brought L.Q.'s mentor Hunter to the forefront of the sectional infighting. Buchanan's cabinet quarreled amongst themselves, while Secretary of War John Buchanan Floyd called on Hunter and James M. Mason to assist him to assuage fears that the fort would be attacked by angry

---

[19]Reprinted by permission of Louisiana State University Press, Entry of August 12, 1860 in Scarborough, ed., *Diary of Edmund Ruffin*, 448.
[20]Ibid.

The Rise of an Insider

South Carolinians.[21] There was no mention of assistance by L.Q. in this matter, but there was evidence that he finally abandoned sectional reconciliation earlier than many Virginians. In mid-January 1861, he wrote his views in a public format-likely a newspaper editorial- and Ruffin noted that L.Q. encouraged the maintenance of "southern principles, & urging co-operative action of the people of Washington with Va & Md, when seceding..."[22]

Washington, D.C. was a most unwelcome place for persons of Southern sentiment in early 1861. It was still a Southern city, but long embroiled with the tension of tugging Unionist sentiment. While L.Q. was hopeful for a rebound of Southern political control of the city, his hopes must surely have been dashed after the February 1861 "Gentleman's Convention." Eminent Upper South representatives, including former President John Tyler, arrived to make last ditch efforts at compromise on the burgeoning regional issues. The aforementioned "Gentleman's Convention," or the Washington Peace Conference of 1861, brought together 132 representatives from different states. Virginia initiated the conference, and it was held without

---

[21] Reprinted by permission of Louisiana State University Press, Entry of August 28, 1860, in Scarborough, ed., *The Diary of Edmund Ruffin*, 451; Philip Gerald Auchampaugh, Ph.D., *James Buchanan and His Cabinet on the Eve of Secession* (Lancaster, PA: privately printed, 1926), 135-136.

[22] Reprinted by permission of Louisiana State University Press, Entry of January 18, 1861, in Scarborough, ed., *The Diary of Edmund Ruffin*, 535-536.

The Rise of an Insider

President Lincoln's knowledge at Willard's Hotel. Unfortunately, the Washington Conference began at the same time that the Confederate Government was forming in Montgomery, Alabama. Both the Confederacy and the Union Governments were vying for Virginia's support. Despite the fact a petition and recommendations from the Washington Conference were drawn up in late February, it never progressed through the House of Representatives.[23]

March 1861 was a crucial month for L.Q. He remained in Washington following the departure of the Southern representatives, and was in the unique position of gathering intelligence for the new Confederate government from "behind the lines" in the seat of the Union government. He reported the actions of the tense city to friends in Richmond and the new Confederate Secretary of War, Leroy Pope Walker. As occupied as he was with these matters, he remained concerned about his friend Hunter's career within the new power structure in the Confederacy. Writing to his friend Lewis E. Harvie, L.Q. stated:

> I quite agree with you as to the absolute necessity that our friends should <u>at once</u> begin an active & a thorough canvass of the State. I have tried to get Mr. Hunter, Mason & others to take the stump....I know that a class of men in our own ranks are now

---

[23]Robert Gray Gunderson, *Old Gentlemen's Convention-The Washington Peace Conference of 1861* (Madison, WI: University of Wisconsin Press, 1961), ix; Ibid., 6; Jesse L. Keene, *The Peace Convention of 1861* (Tuscaloosa, AL: Confederate Publishing Co., Inc., 1961), 116-117.

saying that Hunter and Mason are inactive, and that they are indifferent about the matter. They will try to break them down. If secession is defeated, they will be put out of public life. They can never be the pets of the submissionists.[24]

He urged Hunter that he "ought to speak in Rd [Richmond] at once. Jeff Davis, [Robert] Toombs, & [Robert] Yancey carried their states by work and speaking to the people."[25] In order to ensure his mentor's high office in the new Confederacy, L.Q. hoped Hunter would bolster support for Virginia to join it. Walker and the Confederate Cabinet knew L.Q.'s vital influence on Hunter, and they needed Virginia to make the Confederacy viable. In March 1861, L.Q. was thirty-five years old and held a great deal of power.

Walker maintained an open dialogue with L.Q., beginning from a February 2, 1861 communication to Southerners over the formation of a provisional government in Montgomery. Defining himself as a representative of border state sympathizers, L.Q. said the assembly at Montgomery was interesting to outsiders, but the next weeks were crucial to its survival. He decided that an immediate formation of the provisional government was necessary to alleviate anxiety and confusion in the surrounding states and countries. L.Q. advised, "Do not fear Virginia & the

---

[24]Washington to Lewis E. Harvie, Esq, March 24, 1861, Harvie Family Papers, Virginia Historical Society, Richmond, VA.
[25]Ibid.

The Rise of an Insider

others. Go ahead & all will come right."[26]

Walker took L.Q.'s advice, as he hoped for a vote of secession and wanted the newsman's insight. L.Q. was ready to give ample advice on the early war situations, including the festering situation at Fort Sumter.

> For a week or thereabouts the impression here has been general that the United States Government would withdraw its troops from Sumter, the motive, of course, necessity, as we knew. [Col. Robert] Anderson could not be succored, and he could be starved out in two or three weeks...it is now understood that Fort Pickens is to be retained and defended, and also the Tortugas forts. It is also the opinion of the most sagacious men here that an extra session will be called and Congress asked to furnish additional means for coercion. I have no doubt whatever that the latter is the policy determined on and also that your ministers will be refused a hearing. I trust that the Confederate States will take precisely the same course in respect to the Tortugas as to Fort Pickens and Pensacola.[27]

---

[26] L.Q. Washington to the Editor of the *Mail*, February 2, 1861, M331, Roll 260, Compiled Service Records of Confederate Generals & Staff Officers & Non-Regimental Enlisted Men, 1961, National Archives.

[27] L.Q. Washington to L.P. Walker, March 17, 1861 in *The War of the Rebellion: A Compilation of the Official Records of the Union and Confederate Armies, Series I, Volume LIII* (Washington: Government Printing Office, 1898), 133. The fort opposite island-bound Fort Sumter was Fort Pickens, located on a spit of land just outside Charleston. The Dry Tortugas off Florida were fortified by Fort Jefferson.

The Rise of an Insider

L.Q. was enthusiastic toward the new Southern Confederacy. He tended to be overly positive, but Walker must have found L.Q.'s analysis indicative of Virginia's eventual secession. Equally inspiring were his positive reports toward Virginia's possibility of joining the Confederacy.

> Your Constitution is excellent, and so far the proceedings of your Government have been marked by the very highest statesmanship and wisdom. You have no idea how much benefit they have been to us who in the border States are fighting the battle for a Southern confederacy. Only one thing I desire to caution against: Do not now push the matter looking to slaves coming from the border-States. Virginia, to be moved at all, must not be threatened, and all of that sort of legislation at this time only embarrasses us. As to the border States, I begin to see daylight. The Virginia people voted under the delusion, skillfully planted in their minds by Douglas, Crittenden, and others, that the Crittenden proposition could be obtained...Since this illusion has been dispelled by events, there has been a marked reaction all over the State in favor of secession at once.[28]

L.Q. dashed a second letter off to Walker three days later. He related the Union response to the Fort Sumter quagmire. L.Q.'s intelligence work for Walker was noteworthy in foreshadowing coming actions and the explanation for others just passed, such as

---

[28]Ibid. The Crittenden Compromise, forwarded by Kentucky Congressman John J. Crittenden, failed as did the proposals from the Washington Peace Convention.

The Rise of an Insider

the lost opportunity to take Fort Pickens.

> Several gentlemen not connected with the Government, but who are in the way of getting reliable intelligence, and whom I have always found better informed than any one of my acquaintance, tell me to-day that they have information which satisfied them the Government here means to re-enforce Fort Pickens...Their belief is that the re-enforcement will take place soon...One of the possible steps of this Government may be to direct vessels at sea with troops to make the harbor of Pensacola by a given night and land men and munitions at Fort Pickens... I beg to make this suggestion: When the first step of occupying Fort Pickens was taken by the United States the orders were sent down by a special messenger and also by a telegraph in cipher. The telegraph left here in the night, and was stopped in Mobile or Montgomery by our friends. I gave the fact early next day to the Florida delegation, but the special messenger went through, delivered his message to Lieutenant Slemmer, and thus we lost Fort Pickens.[29]

L.Q. stated in the second Walker letter that Fort Pickens might have been secured, but it was obvious that the same action would get a reaction from South Carolinians watching nearby. Walker's personal secretary, J.J. Hooper, wrote two days later that L.Q. could greatly assist the Confederate forces by incorporating the National Volunteers in its army. Hooper acknowledged the difficult nature of achieving this, and no record exists of L.Q.'s

---

[29] Washington to Walker, March 20, 1861 in *OR*, LII, part II, 27.

The Rise of an Insider

reaction.[30]

Despite his inability to raise troops directly for the Confederacy, L.Q. continued his intelligence reports to Walker. He wrote on April 4th, stating that "a Virginia submissionist came up here the other day to get some pacific assurances from Lincoln and Seward."[31] L.Q. also supplied information on Fort Sumter.

> A gentleman much mixed up with navy officers, of excellent judgment, told me to-day that he was convinced that they intended to re enforce Sumter and Pickens and blockade the mouth of the Mississippi; that the naval officers were all advising coercion, and that there was unusual activity in fitting out vessels for sea. Another gentleman, who sees much of the Cabinet and the Navy Department, expressed the opinion to-day that a war policy was resolved on... I am satisfied that Lincoln's own feelings and theories of duty all run on the side of coercion. It appears to me the Administration is concentrating its resources for a blow.[32]

L.Q. remained confident that Virginia intended to secede, and that coercive action by the North would bring it about. Ever enthusiastic in reporting his movements in Washington to support his opinions, L.Q. wrote again to Walker on April 6th. In this letter, there was a certain alarm sounding in his words.

---

[30]J.J. Hooper to Washington, March 22, 1861 in *OR*, LI, part II, 8.
[31]Washington to Walker, April 4, 1861 in *OR*, LIII, 138.
[32]Ibid.

> I wrote you on the 4th instant by Adams & Co.'s Express, expressing the opinion that the policy of this Government was hostile. The military movements since leave no doubt in my mind as to this. You have probably ere this an account of the formidable armament preparing at New York. They have 2,600 troops ready to start, and nearly every available ship in the Navy has been ordered to prepare for service...Although it is rumored that the expedition is for Santo Domingo, to repel Ampudia's invasion, Key West, &c., yet the opinion of the best informed men here is that Pensacola is the point menaced...I cannot shake off my mind the belief that they have some plan to re-enforce Sumter by means of a combined movement by sea and by land, taking Beauregard's batteries in rear with infantry and field artillery, &c., while their ships press up the bay.[33]

With this letter, L.Q. succeeded where many had not. He scared the prominent men of the Confederate Government. It was improbable that a real attack on Pierre Beauregard's men in Charleston would take place by land, but Walker had little choice but to rely on his intelligence. Besides, L.Q. knew Virginia's secession was imminent in the consequence of war.

> I take it for granted that you have lost no time in getting ready for this state of things. The first news of a conflict will precipitate secession by Virginia. I hope ere it happens the rascally convention

---

[33] Washington to Walker, April 6, 1861 in *OR*, LII, Part II, 37. There was a scare that Hispanic forces were taking advantage of the sectional situation to invade the Florida Keys, but it was an unfounded fear.

will have adjourned, so that it can be done by popular action, and thus get rid of the convention and the Union together.[34]

A week later, the first shots were fired on Fort Sumter. Even then, L.Q.'s influence was silently present in the form of his friend Edmund Ruffin. The secessionist fired the first official cannonade of the American Civil War.[35] Virginia seceded shortly thereafter. The act inflated L.Q.'s reputation despite the fact that there was no real evidence of a land attack.

The onset of war meant that L.Q. had to leave the capitol city and head south for Richmond. The hardest part was separation from his sister Mary, who had married a New Hampshire-born physician, Warwick Evans. The first M.D. graduate of Georgetown College's program in July 1852, Evans was an affluent lecturer and Professor of Anatomy at the institution. His position and a young family kept Mary in Washington, and L.Q.'s open sympathy with the Confederacy made his stay untenable.[36]

---

[34]Ibid. By convention, Washington is speaking of the pro-union convention in Virginia, chaired by unionist John Janney of Loudoun County.

[35]Eric H. Walther, *The Fire-Eaters* (Baton Rouge, LA: Louisiana State University Press, 1992), 265-266.

[36]Pedigree Chart in Ruth Lincoln Kaye, *Hufty and Washington Families* (typescript, February 1997); *A Catalogue of the Officers and Students of Georgetown College, District of Columbia, For the Academic Year 1851-52* (Baltimore, MD: John Murphy & Co., 1852), order of exercises; *History of the Medical Society of the District of*

The Rise of an Insider

The L.Q. Washington who left the nation's capital in early 1861 had matured from a young adventurer to a political insider with considerable power. The power was gained by circumstance, occupation, and location. By leaving home, he made a crucial choice that affected the course of the rest of his life. Yet his pivotal role in March and April 1861 assisted his friends' fortunes as well as his own in the new Confederacy.

Columbia 1817-1909 (Washington, D.C.: Medical Society of the District of Columbia, 1909), 266; John F. Stapleton, M.D., *Upward Journey-The Story of Internal Medicine at Georgetown, 1851-1881* (Washington, D.C.: Georgetown University Medical Center, 1996), 13.

"Grateful for the Offer"

By early 1861 L.Q. Washington had gone south to the Confederacy and a promising future, stating "I promptly quitted my residence in Washington for the purpose of becoming a citizen of this State and aiding her in the struggle then impending."[1] Although well connected to Richmond's editors through his writing, L.Q.'s fiery Southern temperament led him to the military. By April 26th, 1861, a recommendation for an appointment was received for his services. In the early days of the war, the new Confederate Government was still sorting out its initial commands and appointments. It took almost an entire month for L.Q. to receive his commission as a 1st Lieutenant of Infantry.[2]

L.Q. served as Acting Assistant Quartermaster for General Milledge Luke Bonham, joining the command at Camp Pickens in Manassas. He spent a good deal of time with the advance command posted at Fairfax Courthouse, Virginia. The quartermaster's job was a hard one. He was responsible for the logistics of feeding and clothing a large, hungry army, often without the support of his command.[3]

> I have been acting as Quarter Master for Genl Bonham's Command at Centreville for two weeks & am now here as such. I gone on spending money,

---

[1] L.Q. Washington to President Andrew Johnson, June 28, 1865, M1003, Case Files of Applications from Former Confederates for Presidential Pardons ("Amnesty Papers"), 1865-1867, Roll 70, NARA, 1976, National Archives.
[2] Reference card of L.Q. Washington, M331, Roll 260, National Archives.
[3] L.Q. Washington to Confederate President Jefferson Davis, March 11, 1862, M331, National Archives.

"*Grateful for the Offer*"

buying forage & without <u>one cent being advanced to me</u>. My operations & the interests of the army have been & are seriously crippled by this thing....[4]

L.Q.'s work taxed him both financially and physically. He tabulated a constantly shifting account of stores, some purchased, some captured from the enemy. He maintained a detailed list containing the exact numbers of horses, mules, and oxen available for use. He tallied the consumed portion of oats, corn, barley, hay, and fodder, which had to be recalculated on a daily basis. In a statement of forage for June 1861, L.Q. stated in the remarks section that "teams were coming every day & at different times of the day & had to be fed as they came in."[5]

The increase in stores and horses foreshadowed an upcoming military campaign. Union forces in Washington were uncomfortable with the Confederates camping a mere twenty miles away from the Capitol. Bonham's advance line fell back to Fairfax Courthouse, then Centreville. Several skirmishes between the two sides took place at Arlington and Vienna, but the Confederate line retreated slowly westward. There were still periodic raids and the need for horses. On July 8th, L.Q. recorded that Colonel James Lawson Kemper's men confiscated a wagon and two horses with harnesses under the issue of the county court. About the same time, Camp Pickens prepared for a

---

[4] L.Q. Washington to R.M.T. Hunter, June 23, 1861, Papers of R.M.T. Hunter, Reel 7, Hunter-Garnett Family Papers (MSS 38-45), Special Collections Department, University of Virginia Library.
[5] Statement of Forage, No. 34, June 1861, M331, Roll 260, National Archives.

"Grateful for the Offer"

long siege by ordering hatchets, nails, and even oilstones by the end of June.[6]

The following days saw Union advances and increased stores activity. After some initial skirmishes, Union General Irwin McDowell sent his corps picketing westward. It was a slow advance, for L.Q. was still stationed at Fairfax Courthouse on July 13th when he received a sizable order of envelopes, paper, and ink. However, Union troops finally forced Confederate forces to pull back on about July 16th. That day L.Q. received quartermasters' funds totaling two thousand dollars, for which L.Q. was accountable. Union forces approached Fort Pickens by the 18th, when L.Q.'s records showed that a saddle and bridle were taken from captured troops around Bull Run.[7]

The Battle of First Manassas, or Bull Run, on the 21st proved a decisive Confederate victory. It enshrined the reputations of General Thomas J. "Stonewall" Jackson, Colonel Nathan Evans, General Bernard Bee, and countless others. Although McDowell's men held out most of the day, they broke under an afternoon assualt and fled in panic towards the Capitol.[8]

---

[6]Abstract of Articles, No. 45, Quarter Ended 30th September, 1861, Attachment N, M331, Roll 260, National Archives; Requisition for Stores Manassas Junction, June 1861, M331, Roll 260, National Archives.
[7]Abstract No. 29, List of Stores Transferred to Lt. L.Q. Washington, July 13, 1861, M331, Roll 260, National Archives; Voucher Transferred to Lt. L.Q. Washington, July 16, 1861, M331, Roll 260, National Archives; Abstract of Articles, No. 45, M331, Roll 260, National Archives.
[8] "Historical Sketch of the Rockbridge Artillery, C.S. Army, by a Member of the Famous Battery," in *Southern Historical Society Papers, Vol. XXIII* (Broadfoot Publishing Co., 1991, Reprint), 112-113;

"Grateful for the Offer"

Following the Battle of Manassas, the quartermaster had to inventory the incredible amount of captured stores. In addition, he monitored large scale spending for food and forage for the new pickets. The preparations before and after the Battle of Manassas wore L.Q. down. He preferred the duties of Assistant Adjutant General and wrote his former boss, powerful Confederate statesman James Murray Mason, requesting to be transferred to that staff in Manassas permanently. Mason wrote back that he had spoken to Confederate President Jefferson Davis on L.Q.'s behalf. In order to obtain a transfer to the Provisional Army as Assistant Adjutant General, L.Q. resigned his commission as 1st Lieutenant of Infantry on August 13th. His official resignation of the Acting Assistant Quartermaster's position was made on August 23rd, and was accepted August 27th. In a strange twist of fate, Davis suffered one of his sudden sick periods shortly thereafter, leaving incomplete L.Q.'s transfer. For three months, L.Q. served as a regular soldier in the Confederate forces. Unsure of the future of his position with the Confederate forces, L.Q. went to Richmond to wait until an appropriate time to obtain an interview with Davis.[9]

In early September, L.Q. was in Richmond settling his accounts from his previous service. He submitted quarterly returns for the second and third quarters on September 6th,

---

Ibid., 116.
[9]L.Q. Washington to Jefferson Davis, March 11, 1862, M331, Roll 260, National Archives; Typed statement of service, L. Quinton Washington, M331, Roll 260, National Archives; L.Q. Washington to Quartermaster General, Richmond, VA, September 6, 1861, M331, Roll 260, National Archives.

apologizing to his superior about the delay in submission. He stated that, "It arose from circumstances beyond my control, from a great pressure of current business and the difficulties consequent upon an advance position, and from the fact that I had no clerk who understood how to prepare the accounts."[10]

L.Q. settled his accounts, but there remained another problem; he was still unemployed. Without a commission or interview with Davis, he had no choice but to seek other avenues of employment. An opportunity arose when *Richmond Examiner* editor John Moncure Daniel chose to serve in the Confederate army. L.Q. was familiar with Daniel's journalistic reputation. He was the editor of the *Examiner* since 1847 and ruffled many feathers as only a newsman could. Once the famed Edgar Allen Poe challenged the aggressive Daniel to a duel. The *Examiner*'s prominence under Daniel continued right into the first months of the Civil War until he enlisted. In some good timing, L.Q. assumed the position of Editor-in-Chief of the *Richmond Examiner* for a time. His employment did not last long; by November Daniel had returned to Richmond to resume control of the *Examiner*.[11]

L.Q. again sought political appointment. He turned to his old friend Robert M.T. Hunter, who was serving as Acting

---

[10] Washington to Quartermaster General, September 6, 1861, M331, Roll 260, National Archives.
[11] J. Cutler Andrews, *The South Reports the Civil War*, Copyright @ 1970 by Princeton University Press, Reprinted by permission of Princeton University Press, 30; Virginius Dabney, *Pistols and Pointed Pens-The Dueling Editors of Old Virginia* (Chapel Hill, NC: Algonquin Books of Chapel Hill, 1987), 39-43. There is very little mention of what transpired during Washington's brief stay.

"Grateful for the Offer"

Confederate Secretary of State for the departed Robert Toombs. Hunter gave L.Q. the Chief Clerkship in his department on November 4, 1861. The job was interesting. He issued passports to citizens wanting to travel beyond the boundaries of the Confederacy and to those observing the war from abroad. In addition, L.Q. was privy to important foreign relations activity and was a primary contact between couriers and the Confederate Government. He also gave his supervisor regular updates on foreign sentiment, generally gathered from agents and news sources. As long as Hunter remained as Acting Secretary of State, L.Q. felt secure in his position.[12]

There were times that L.Q. showed insecurity. Writing about the Civil War in September 1901, L.Q. noted the scarcity of written accounts or duties of the Confederate State Department. Some recollections were surprising, such as L.Q.'s concern for Jefferson Davis' safety.[13]

He was at this time confined to his home on Shockoe Hill by a protracted illness, but he possessed a great vitality and he recovered in a month or so. After that illness he was careful to take regular exercise. He used to take very long rides in the country, going out late in the evening and having only a single

---

[12]Washington to President Johnson, June 28, 1865, M1003, National Archives; L.Q. Washington Oath of Office, November 4, 1861, Pickett Papers, Reel 25, Library of Congress Manuscripts Division.

[13]L.Q. Washington, "Confederate States State Department. A Description of It by Colonel L.Q. Washington," in R.A. Brock, ed., *Southern Historical Society Papers, Volume XXIX* (Richmond, VA: Southern Historical Society, 1901), 347. Reprint by Broadfoot Publishing, 1991.

"Grateful for the Offer"

companion, perhaps one of his aids, or his sister-in-law, Miss Howell. The country about Richmond was at that time thickly wooded, imperfectly guarded, and he ran considerable risk, but on a point like that he would not have relished advice.[14]

L.Q.'s occupational reunion with Hunter did not last. In the final months of 1861, Hunter's allies urged him to enter the Confederate Senate as a representative of Virginia. Hunter was more comfortable with the subject of finance, perhaps feeling that a position as the leading diplomat of the Confederacy was not a permanent goal. Nevertheless, Hunter ran for office and was easily elected. On February 22, 1862, he formally vacated the Confederate State Department.[15]

The day was noteworthy in Richmond. February 22, 1862 was the day the "Permanent Constitution," as L.Q. described it, was formally established. This document finalized the framework of the Confederate Government. Secretary of War Judah P. Benjamin took over the office of the Confederate Secretary of State. Hunter's Assistant Secretary of State, William M. Browne, became an aide to Jefferson Davis. As chief clerk, L.Q. knew he might be moved as well. In March, he wrote Davis of his concern.[16]

> Being disengaged I accepted office of employment which, when I took them, promised a field of usefulness. The post now held by me, as Chief Clerk of the State Department, is one of high honor and trust; but in holding it, at this time, I cannot feel that

---

[14]Ibid.
[15]Ibid., 348.
[16]Ibid., 343-344.

"Grateful for the Offer"

> I am contributing to the great cause in which we are embarked. My earnest desire is to give my time and best energies to the country during the war. Actuated by this aim I have submitted this statement in the hope that, if you deem me worthy, you may be able to assign me some position in the Army where I may serve usefully and share the risks which others are meeting.[17]

L.Q. was neither removed from the State Department nor given an assignment in the Confederate army. While it may be assumed that Benjamin felt the stability within his department necessitated L.Q.'s reappointment, there was no mention of the reason for the extension. With Hunter and Browne gone, Washington's presence provided stability in the transition of a department.

Judah Benjamin was an interesting man to L.Q., who wrote of him later as "...a man of society, his tact in personal intercourse was unfailing, his politeness invariable. In all the trials and anxieties of the great struggle, I never saw his temper ruffled or embittered."[18] L.Q. occupied the office next to Benjamin, who arrived daily at nine o'clock and worked until three in the afternoon most days. They regularly met for one hour during the day, but it was Benjamin who personally brought Jefferson Davis important intelligence on the ongoing operations of the State

---

[17] Washington to Davis, March 11, 1862, in M331, Roll 260, National Archives.

[18] Pierce Butler, *Judah P. Benjamin* (Philadelphia, PA: George W. Jacobs & Company, 1906), 330. Gathered from the manuscript material gathered by Englishman Francis Lawley. Lawley was doing so for a planned biography of Benjamin in the 1870s, which never happened.

Department. L.Q. noted that, under Benjamin's tenure, he attended no formal dinners by the cabinet. They lived "very plainly." Benjamin roomed at Richmond's west end with a group of Louisiana Congressmen and his brother-in-law, Jules St. Martin. With his wife in France and other relatives in New Orleans, Benjamin had plenty of time for work.[19]

L.Q.'s work during this period was consistent and painstaking. Note after note had to be issued in copybooks. In addition there were constant requests from individuals and businesses to enter and leave the Confederacy. Benjamin and L.Q. split a good number of these official requests. In granting papers, L.Q. kept informed on all major events during the war.

> The important military news came to us, of course, and also many of the plans of military operations. I had so many friends in Congress that I easily kept advised of what it was doing. On the other hand, no one on the outside knew the business of the State Department except the President, and he was not the kind of a man to gossip or be questioned.[20]

The "important military news" during early 1862 ranged from desperate pleas for foreign aid to McClellan's U.S. Army inching their way up the York River towards Richmond. First hand reports were highly valuable since, according to L.Q.'s account, Benjamin had some trouble directing certain operations as he had to rely upon "Northern or on foreign newspapers, since the press of the South was suffering from the same stoppage of

---

[19]Ibid., 330-334.
[20]Washington, "Confederate States State Department," in *Southern Historical Society Papers, XXIX*, 344.

communication...and these outside sources of information might well be regarded with suspicion, sometimes of ignorance..."[21] L.Q. gave Horace Greeley's *New York Tribune* as an example of the kind of biased journalism which had minimal intelligence value to the Confederate officials. Instead the State Department turned to foreign papers such as the *London Times* and *Daily Telegraph*. Even *Blackwood's Magazine* was scoured by State Department operatives in England. As a former journalist, L.Q. undoubtedly knew the best papers upon which to rely.[22]

Great Britain was an important factor in the early stages of the Civil War. The United States Navy captured the English steamer *Trent* in December 1861, whose passengers included the Confederate ministers to England and France, James M. Mason and John Slidell. The British Government furiously demanded the ministers to be released and their coffers compensated for their trouble. Following a standoff, Mason and Slidell were freed. However, tensions between the Federals and Great Britain remained. Benjamin used his best intelligence to exploit the tension and achieve British recognition for the Confederacy. In writing early dispatches on the subject to Mason and London Agent Henry Hotze, Benjamin labored in long phrases with little effort to draft them. L.Q. noted that Benjamin "had the art to hide. I have known him often to compose a long dispatch or State paper with great rapidity, with hardly a word changed or

---

[21] John S. Bowman, ed., *The Civil War Day by Day* (Greenwich, CT: Dorset Press, Brompton Books, 1989), 70-71; Butler, *Benjamin*, 292.
[22] Ibid., 293.

"Grateful for the Offer"

interlined..."[23]

Despite these grand efforts, events in England were developing slowly. By late summer 1862, despite Confederate victories at Second Manassas and the Seven Days' Campaign, Britain was hesitant to be involved. Then New Orleans fell to the Union forces in spring 1862, revealing that the South had a soft underbelly.[24]

Another vital diplomatic tie for the Confederacy was France. With French-based Louisiana deeply rooted in Southern traditions, there was already a fairly strong bond with Paris. A rumor circulated after the war that Benjamin's friend, Duncan Kenner, offered the French the state of Louisiana in exchange for direct intervention by the French Government under Emperor Louis Napoleon. L.Q. himself quashed that rumor in 1901, stating "perhaps this is the proper place to say that the secrets of the Confederate Government were well kept...It was hatched at a time when gossip was easy..."[25]

The society surrounding Benjamin and his cohorts gave L.Q. unrestricted access to the "inner circles" of political power. His office at the Treasury Building along Bank Street allowed L.Q. to

---

[23]Bowman, ed., *Civil War Day by Day*, 46-48; Thomas H. Flaherty et al, eds., *The Blockade-Runners and Raiders* (Alexandria, VA: Time-Life Books, 1983), 116-117; Robert Douthat Meade, *Judah P. Benjamin-Confederate Statesman*, Copyright @1943, Oxford University Press, New York, NY, Reprinted by Permission of Oxford University Press, 260.
[24]Meade, *Benjamin*, 260-262.
[25]Ibid., 264; Washington, "Confederate States State Department," *Southern Historical Society Papers*, 342.

"Grateful for the Offer"

meet many famous people of the time.²⁶ One such personality was the famous diarist Mary Boykin Chesnut. She noted meeting L.Q. on several occasions, the first from an entry on April 21st, 1862. Chesnut was ill at the time, and frightened by advancing Union troops near Yorktown. She relayed her happiness upon receiving a letter "from Quinton Washington. That was the best tonic yet. He writes so cheerfully. We have fifty thousand men on the Peninsula and McClellan eighty thousand. We expect that much disparity of numbers. We can stand that."²⁷

As Richmond was in danger of invasion, talk of society and battle were intertwined. When General George B. McClellan's Union troops advanced toward Richmond, L.Q. was resolute in his belief that Richmond would not fall. Chesnut noted in her entry of May 18, 1862, about L.Q.'s calculation of odds.

> Very encouraging letters from Hon. [Treasury Secretary] Mr. Memminger and from L.Q. Washington. They tell me the same story in very different words. It amounts to this: "Not one foot of Virginia soil is to be given up without a bitter fight for it. We have one hundred and five thousand

---

[26] *An Official Guide of the Confederate Government From 1861 to 1865 at Richmond-Showing the Location of the Public Buildings and Offices of the Confederate, State and City Governments, Residences of the Principal Officers, etc.* (unknown: Ricketts Associates, 1981), 2.

[27] Entry of April 21st in Isabella D. Martin and Myrta Lockett Avary, eds, *A Diary from Dixie, as written by Mary Boykin Chesnut, wife of James Chesnut, Jr., United States Senator from South Carolina, 1859-1861, and afterward an Aide to Jefferson Davis and a Brigadier-General in the Confederate Army*, Peter Smith Publisher, Inc., Gloucester, MA, 1929, 157-158. From this entry, it is evident that Chesnut met Washington before the entry.

"Grateful for the Offer"

men in all, McClellan one hundred and ninety thousand. We can stand that disparity."[28]

L.Q. was correct in his calculations. The Seven Days' Battles, which came perilously close to Richmond, proved that familiarity of ground compensated for numbers. At Malvern Hill, General Robert E. Lee's men pinned McClellan's army against the James River. A short time later the Union forces left the area. It appeared the disparity was balanced.[29]

Following McClellan's withdrawal, the Confederate Government shifted back into its original routine. L.Q. dealt with matters of state in regard to domestic affairs. In answering one letter regarding the Union army's seizure of slaves, L.Q. dealt with the angry slave owners in a delicate and tactful manner, as Southern planters viewed their slaves as they did their gold. Much of the Southern planter's wealth was invested in the slave system, and the Union presence along the South Carolina coast brought about the periodic capture of those slaves and other property. L.Q. was forced to deal with the issue of compensation for such losses, as he did in a reply to Captain Horace H. Sams, Hardeeville, South Carolina:

> Your letter of the 26th Sept has been received enclosing testimony taken in the matter of slaves and other property seized by the enemy, with a request for a certified copy agreeably to the terms of the Act of Congress Aug 30th 1861. The certified copy will be sent upon your forwarding to the Department the sum of $1.00 to pay--for seal and

---

[28] Entry of May 18th in Martin and Avary, ed., *A Diary from Dixie*, 164.
[29] Bowman, ed., *Civil War Day by Day*, 74-75.

copy here. I suggest to you that it would be best for you to forward a duplicate of the paper you have already sent with the addition that the judicial office shall state in his certificate of authentication that the "evidence so heard and transmitted is entitled to credit."[30]

Foreign affairs took much time during this period. Benjamin and L.Q. again sought British and French recognition, but many issues were pending in late 1862. Noting the need for Southern cotton, there was a good chance that both European powers would recognize the Confederacy following the Seven Days' Battles. Benjamin sent John Slidell instructions to exchange war materials for duty-free shipping of French products into the Confederacy. However, further instruction reached Slidell slowly. He made a proposal in late July that the Confederacy could assist France in a proposed conquest of Mexico. Emperor Napoleon III attempted to get British and Russian support to solidify the agreement.[31]

A flurry of diplomacy, emphasizing British support, followed in the Autumn of 1862. Richmond directly pressured British officials in late 1862. A Confederate victory at Second Manassas and the eventual advance of the Army of Northern Virginia into Maryland ensured a reaction from Europe. However, the Confederates narrowly avoided disaster at Sharpsburg in October 1862. The battle played on the minds of the British ministers.[32]

---

[30]L.Q. Washington to Captain Horace H. Sams, September 30th, 1862, "Pickett Papers," Container 22, Reel 13, 235, Library of Congress Manuscripts.
[31]Meade, *Benjamin*, 253; Ibid., 255-256.
[32]Ibid., 254; Ibid., 257.

"Grateful for the Offer"

Despite the precarious situation, Benjamin and L.Q. handled the issues as they arose. Some support came from foreign military efforts. L.Q. wrote to British Consul Robert Bunch about the recruitment of British Confederate soldiers.

> I am instructed by the Secretary of State of the Confederate States to acknowledge receipt of your letter of 12th inst. communicating to him views on the subject of enrolling certain English born soldiers in the Army of the Confederacy, which views you are instructed by Earl [John] Russell to signify to the Secretary as those of Her Majesty's Government.[33]

New rounds of diplomacy failed after Sharpsburg. Earl Russell declined Emperor Napoleon's call for mutual support on December 1, 1862. Without Britain, Napoleon was less apt to recognize the Confederacy alone. He was still warm to Confederate officials, but lowered his level of assistance. All European support to the Confederacy was gone save easy access to private loans.[34]

L.Q. gathered the freshest intelligence reference material for State Department use, especially in light of future attempts at foreign recognition. He wrote to operative George N. Sanders on December 8th:

> You are authorized to procure and forward to this Department for its use the following documents, papers, &c:

---

[33] L.Q. Washington to Robert Bunch Esq, November 17th, 1862 in Papers of the Confederate State Department, "Pickett Papers", Container 22, Reel 13, 257, Library of Congress Manuscripts.
[34] Meade, *Benjamin*, 257; Ibid., 268-270.

1. The Continuation of the volumes of U.S. State on foreign relations-that is, all subsequent to the four volumes on that head, published by Gales & Seaton. If these cannot be had bound, they may be sent unbound.
2. The U.S. Census Compendium of 1860, or if not, had then the last three numbers of the American Almanac.
3. The laws of the United States and decisions of the U.S. Supreme Court and Congressional Globes of Lincoln Administration.
4. The U.S. Presidents Message of 1862 and accompanying Documents, to wit that relative to foreign affairs.
5. Tribune Almanacs of 1862 and 1863.
6. Last U.S. Blue Book and Army and Naval Regulations issued by United States.
7. The last British Blue Book on Foreign Affairs.
8. The Edinburg Quarterly and Westminster Review, and Blackwood's Magazine.
9. The Times, Post Herald and Saturday Review
For the delivery of these you will be paid by the Department.[35]

In addition to gathering information for an archive, L.Q. was a confidante to Benjamin. Besides occupying an office next to the Secretary, L.Q. had knowledge of secret information. This was evident in a letter received and answered in December 1862, when he learned of the British inclination to intervene in the Civil War. The State Department's agent in Nassau, a man named Heylinger, wrote to Benjamin's attention on December 15th:

---

[35] L.Q. Washington to George N. Sanders, December 8th, 1862, "Pickett Papers," Container 22, Reel 13, 267, Library of Congress Manuscripts. Washington knew Gales and Seaton from his old days in Washington. He would later work for the *London Telegraph*.

"Grateful for the Offer"

> The British ships of war Melssomene, Cadmus & Peterol have been sent to Charleston to watch proceedings. I learn again that the attack is to be made in Christmas week. The British frigates Immortalite and Orlando are stationed at Matamoros, and the Rinaldo remains at N. Orleans.[36]

L.Q. copied the letter into official journals and, after discussing it with Benjamin, it was decided to redirect the information to James A. Seddon, the Confederate Secretary of War. On December 25th, an official letter was forwarded under L.Q.'s name for Seddon's use. While this particular letter never made history, L.Q.'s access to sensitive information was evident.[37]

In early 1863, L.Q.'s attention centered on several key issues. Although he continued the endless struggle for European recognition of the Confederacy, emphasis within the Confederate State Department shifted to more internal issues, such as state safety. L.Q. noted the formation of a small garrison to protect Richmond.[38] The issue of spies operating within the city gave L.Q. little worry. Their information, according to L.Q., was inaccurate. He wrote years later that the famed Unionist Elizabeth Van Lew was known to be a Northern sympathizer. She had "no official position or social entre, contrived to purvey highly important information for the Washington Government.

---

[36] L. Heylinger to Hon. J.P. Benjamin, 15 December 1862, M437, Letters Received by the Confederate War Department, Roll 79, Frame 498, National Archives.

[37] L.Q. Washington to Hon. J.A. Seddon, December 25, 1862, M437, Roll 79, Frame 497, National Archives.

[38] "Confederate States State Department," *Southern Historical Society Papers, Volume XXIX*, 343.

"Grateful for the Offer"

She might have picked up some empty gossip and rumors in circulation, but nothing more."³⁹

Such statements indicated that L.Q. was either naive or well informed. Given his knowledge of detailed incidents such as the possible attack on Charleston, it was likely the latter.

In his chief clerk position, L.Q. was able to assist other Confederate departments on a variety of levels. One such example was in April 1863, when L.Q. wrote to Secretary of War James Seddon about restoring the rank to a soldier.

> Having learned that Captain Chas. K. Sherman is applying to be re-instated in his former rank, I beg leave to state from intimate personal knowledge that he is an accomplished, useful & zealous officer. He took sides early with the South left his home, and has throughout exhibited a devotion to the cause such as is not often found.⁴⁰

L.Q. may not have actually known this soldier, but the parallels to his own situation were apparent.

The bulk of L.Q.'s duties remained with a decision to allow exemptions on citizens' movement to and from the Confederacy. He answered one such request in late July 1863 on a conditional basis.

> Mr Wm Mathews, lately a citizen of California desires to go to Nassau. Having only recently come to the Confederacy he is not entitled to a passport, but if not subject to military duty & I believe he is not there can be no objection to his being allowed to

---

³⁹Ibid.
⁴⁰L.Q. Washington to Hon. J.A. Seddon, April 10th, 1863, M437, Roll 110, National Archives.

"Grateful for the Offer"

leave by way of Wilmington or Charleston.[41]

Tight security was applied in other ways. Foreign vessels of trade, usually European, ran the blockade of northern vessels. They were questioned for potential information. Although L.Q. followed procedure, he found the intelligence gathering a large waste of time. He wrote in 1901,

> The blockade runners were allowed to pass between Richmond and Washington, but were a harmless set of gentlemen. I used to cross-examine them, but met only one that had any intelligence of interest, and that was on subjects not connected with the war. This person was a woman who knew how to use her eyes and ears, but not well enough to affect a campaign or change the face of history.[42]

Equally distressing was Union cavalry probes on Richmond's security. L.Q. was occasionally surprised by raids. When Union General George Stoneman's May 1863 raid toward Richmond was launched, L.Q. was dining at the Chesnut house. Mary Chesnut illustrated this incident in her diary.

> At home I found L.Q. Washington, who stayed to dinner. I saw that he and my husband were intently preoccupied by some event which they did not see

---

[41]L.Q. Washington to General Jno. H. Winder, July 29th, 1863, M437, Roll 104, Frame 74, National Archives.

[42]Washington, "Confederate States State Department," *Southern Historical Society Papers, Vol. XXIX*, 343. It is possible Washington was referring to actress Rose Greenhow, who traveled frequently by ship. She perished during a storm at sea in 1864.

> fit to communicate to me. Immediately after dinner my husband lent Mr. Washington one of his horses and they rode off together. I betook myself to my kind neighbors, the Pattons, for information. There I found Colonel Patton had gone, too. Mrs. Patton, however, knew all about the trouble. She said there was a raiding party within forty miles of us and no troops were in Richmond![43]

The raid failed to reach Richmond, but unrest in the city was rife. In early April 1863, the city's poorer women revolted against the high price of food. They broke shop windows along Cary Street and a full riot appeared to be forthcoming. Only the arrival of Jefferson Davis staved off further looting. A Confederate victory at Chancellorsville bolstered confidence to invade the North, and thus averted away from hard times.[44]

In July 1863, following the tragic loss at Gettysburg, Pennsylvania, the Confederacy went into a period of retrenchment. While routine work continued in Richmond, a personal war incident drew L.Q.'s attention. One of his close friends, Major John Blair Harvie, called on L.Q. to be his second in a duel over a matter of honor between Harvie and Colonel William E. Peters in late 1863. L.Q. handled the duty of messenger between the parties from his Richmond residence. A confusion concerning Colonel Peters' whereabouts led to a delay in arrangements, and on October 26th, 1863 L.Q. penned a

---

[43]Chesnut, *A Diary From Dixie*, 244-245.
[44]Meade, *Benjamin*, 282.

"Grateful for the Offer"

scathing notice to Peters.[45]

> More than ten days has now elapsed since I handed you Major Harvie's challenge, and no reply of any sort from you has been received. Both Major Harvie and his friends have been put to much inconvenience in this effort to obtain satisfaction: first, by the journey raised necessary by your early departure after the insult was given, and now your delay in responding to his note.[46]

The urgent tone of L.Q.'s letter left Peters little choice. He had to respond or face a compromised reputation. Returning a letter dated the same day, Peters acidly commented on the lengthy time elapsed between initial contact and the second letter. Colonel Peters refused to answer Harvie's challenge "until I have accomplished the task I have immediately at hand--When I am ready to do so and when my friend is ready."[47] He complained he had to resign his seat in the state's legislature and could not let it go unfilled.[48]

The arrangements for the duel developed slowly in a second exchange of letters. On the 2nd of November, L.Q. received a letter from Colonel Peter's friend, Dr. A.C. Clendinen, who asked to meet at his room at number 69 Ballard House. They did not meet that night, as the following day another short note was sent

---

[45] L.Q. Washington to Col. Wm E. Peters, October 26th, 1863, L.Q. Washington Papers, Virginia Historical Society.
[46] Ibid.
[47] Col. William E. Peters to L.Q. Washington, October 26th, 1863, L.Q. Washington Papers, Virginia Historical Society.
[48] Ibid.

"Grateful for the Offer"

to L.Q. stating, "For reasons, hereafter to be explained, it would be agreeable to Col. Peters if Major Harvie would withdraw his challenge of the 15th October."[49] L.Q. refused. On the 4th, Clendinen wrote L.Q. that an unnamed source "entitled to the highest respect and confidence" told Colonel Peters that he had been in error and regretted his action. L.Q. took this message as a half-apology, but such an explanation was not acceptable as terms of settlement in order to avert the duel. He wrote Clendinen that "Major Harvie is prepared to afford Col. Peters full opportunity for the tender of a satisfactory apology."[50]

Colonel Peters was not willing to formally apologize to avert a duel. He sent a short note to Major Harvie, stating the doctor was to arrange terms of the contest.[51] On the morning of November 5th, L.Q. wrote Doctor Clendinen to finalize a meeting place and choice of weapons. He was agitated at Colonel Peters for picking at terms on the choice of a weapon.

---

[49] Printed letters of A. Clendinen to Washington, November 2, 1863; A.C. Clendenin to Washington, November 3, 1863 in "Correspondence," *Richmond Enquirer*, December 2, 1863. Included of L.Q. Washington Papers, Virginia Historical Society.
[50] Printed letters of Washington to Dr. A.C. Clendinen, November 3, 1863; A. Clendinen to Washington, November 3, 1863; Washington to Dr. A. Clendinen, November 4, 1863 in "Correspondence," *Richmond Enquirer*, L.Q. Washington Papers, Virginia Historical Society.
[51] Printed letter, William E. Peters to Major J.B. Harvie, November 4, 1863, in "Correspondence," *Richmond Enquirer*, December 2, 1863 in L.Q. Washington Papers, Virginia Historical Society.

"Grateful for the Offer"

> Col. Peters, having yesterday accepted Major Harvie's challenge, of 15th October, and designated you as his friend to arrange the terms of meeting, I had expected you promptly to name the weapon Colonel Peters means to use; but, to my surprise, Colonel Peters, after delaying for twenty days his acceptance of the challenge, still keeps to himself the secret of the weapon to be employed in the combat...I am willing to take rifles, as you have suggested, and I now call on you to fix upon that or some other weapon at once, and to say how it is to be used on the field. You have no right to keep this back to the last moment.[52]

Not only was a weapon an issue, but the location of the duel as well. In this haggling, Washington felt the negotiations were meant to stop the duel.[53] Nevertheless, the terms of the duel were finished on November 5th, and the Harvie-Peters duel occurred on the morning of November 10th, 1863. At sixty yards, both men turned and fired their rifles. Both missed. A field conference between the seconds after the first shot brought about a formal apology from Colonel Peters through his advisors. The duel was over, but as a final act Washington published the exchange of letters in the Richmond papers early the following month. The entire process of arranging the duel took two months of L.Q.'s time.[54]

---

[52] Printed letter, Washington to Dr. A. Clendinen, November 5, 1863, in "Correspondence."

[53] Printed letters Washington to Clendinen, November 5, 1863; A. Clendinen to Washington in "Correspondence."

[54] "Statement of the occurrences on the field. between Col. Wm E. Peters and Major John B. Harvie, Tuesday, 10th November, 1863." in *Richmond Enquirer*, December 2, 1863, in L.Q.

"Grateful for the Offer"

Despite the sidelights around Richmond, the early months of 1864 marked the turning point of L.Q. Washington's fortunes. L.Q. was homesick for his sister and her family. There had been little word between the lines. L.Q. privately wrote his friend R.M.T. Hunter, enquiring if he was wise to send a letter there. Hunter advised caution, but he was curious if it would make it past Federal authorities.[55]

L.Q. was not the only correspondent trying to infiltrate the North; Confederate officials were focused on reaching an anxious public in the interior of the North and exploring possible sympathies. Secretary of State Benjamin had ideas concerning probing Southern sentiment in the North. Beyond sending letters, he wanted to test the loyalty of the citizens. In 1863, activity of the Southern sympathizers or objectors to the war was particularly rampant in the Midwest. Clement Vallandigham, the apparent leader of the objectors in the North, went into exile in Canada. Secretary Benjamin wanted to probe the New England states, and believed solid representation from the Confederacy in Canada might achieve results. To lead a massive propaganda campaign for the Confederacy in Canada, Benjamin first offered the position to Virginian Alexander H.H. Stuart in late March 1864. The talks were sensitive and Stuart was summoned to Richmond rather than risk any interception of passing letters. Benjamin asked Stuart to initiate a small commission office that

---

Washington Papers, Virginia Historical Society.
[55]R.M.T. Hunter to L.Q. Washington, February 22, 1864, Washington Family Papers, Manuscript Division, Library of Congress.

"Grateful for the Offer"

provided monetary aid to Confederate sympathizers.[56] Stuart detailed the offer after the war.

> He [Benjamin] said that the President and himself had agreed upon me as a Commissioner of the Confederate States. The plan was that I should sail to Nassau and thence to Canada. Arrived there, I should have a sort of diplomatic family or court, the mission of which, by which, by means of a secret service, would be to foster and give direct aid to a peace sentiment which it was understood was then active along the Border States...[57]

Stuart declined. Benjamin then assigned the office to two men, former U.S. Secretary of Interior Jacob Thompson and Alabamian Clement C. Clay.[58]

The actual instructions by Davis and Benjamin were revealed in a short descriptive account by L.Q. after the war. There were boundaries to the assignment given to Thompson and Clay, according to the account. Present at the meeting were Thompson, Davis, Benjamin, and L.Q., who wrote:

> I was present at the time when Mr. Thompson received his instructions from Mr. Benjamin. They were oral and largely suggestive and informal. Much was left to his discretion and wisely; for he was an experienced and conservative man. But

---

[56] Frank L. Klement, *The Copperheads in the Middle West* (Chicago: University of Chicago Press, 1960), 94-95; Meade, *Benjamin*, 299-301.
[57] Alexander F. Robertson, *Alexander Hugh Holmes Stuart-A Biography* (Richmond: William Byrd Press, Inc., Printers, 1925), 207.
[58] Klement, *The Copperheads in the Middle West*, 94-95; Meade, *Benjamin*, 299-301.

> there was not a word or a thought that looked to
> any violations of the rules of war, as they exist,
> among civilized nations. As a matter of fact, Mr.
> Davis, Mr. Benjamin, General Lee and the other
> leaders of the Confederacy believed to the last that
> it was not merely right, but the wisest and best policy
> to maintain and respect every one of the humane
> restrictions in the conduct of war...[59]

Thompson had a large bank account and freedom to forge an independent strategy. The months that followed brought serious problems to light. Contact was made with a sympathetic group, the Sons of Liberty, to establish a "Northwest Confederacy." However, Vallandigham was cool towards the official plan. Other similar attempts failed.[60]

Communication by courier between Canada and Richmond was dangerous. It fell to local Canadian operatives to keep account of the plans. L.Q. was abreast of the affairs through one of the couriers, Lewis Sanders. L.Q. wrote the Provost Marshal at Richmond:

> Mr. Lewis Sanders who will present this note
> informs me that [missing] brings a confidential
> communication to the President on public business.
> He has lately been residing in Canada. Will you
> be pleased to give him a passport for week from

---

[59] L.Q. Washington to Lawley, Pierce Butler Papers, Manuscripts Department, Tulane University Library, as quoted in Evans, *Benjamin*, 271-272.
[60] Meade, *Benjamin*, 302-303.

"Grateful for the Offer"

this date [August 11, 1864].[61]

A few months after this communication, an abortive attempt was made to set fires in New York City. Fire was used as a weapon against the South in both Georgia and Virginia's Shenandoah Valley. The sympathizers in New York botched the job, and the scare soon passed for the city residents. There was a notable raid on the town of St. Albans, Vermont in October 1864. While the raid proved more successful than the fire attempts in New York, the two events were the culminations of the Confederate Canadian operations.[62]

The Confederacy was in a desperate political situation when Thompson attempted these latter plans. Georgia fell as General William Tecumseh Sherman worked his way to Savannah. General Lee fought a huge Union army under General Ulysses S. Grant near Petersburg, Virginia. Richmond was in direct danger if Petersburg fell. There remained few diplomatic options left for the Confederate State Department. Duncan Kenner went to Europe to press for direct aid in exchange for the emancipation of slaves.[63]

L.Q. was involved in the diplomacy surrounding the summit to end the war in the first months of 1865, the Hampton Roads Peace Conference. He personally brought the official appointments for the Commissioners representing the South:

---

[61]L.Q. Washington to Col. Carrington, August 11, 1864 in Pickett Papers, Reel 13, Library of Congress Manuscripts.
[62]Meade, *Benjamin,* 303-305.
[63]Ibid., 309-310.

"Grateful for the Offer"

Robert M.T. Hunter, Judge John A. Campbell, and Confederate Vice-President Alexander Stephens. He arrived through the Federal lines during the night, also bringing the currency necessary for the expenses of the Commissioners.[64] The secret conference went through several tiers of communication. Francis P. Blair was President Lincoln's representative. The Commissioners arrived at Grant's Headquarters at City Point, Virginia. Upon arrival, Colonel William Eckert met them with a copy of the appointment letter to Blair. General Grant joined the group shortly. He was impressed with the results and telegraphed Lincoln that the conference proved beneficial. A decision was made for further talks at Hampton Roads. Lincoln and Secretary of State William Seward met with Stephens and Hunter. Although goodwill abounded, no terms could be made without the complete dismantling of the Southern Confederacy.[65]

The eventual failure at Hampton Roads meant desperate attempts at stabilizing the Confederacy. Benjamin openly supported the arming of slaves, which cost him politically. Virginia delegates publicly asked for the resignations of the Confederate cabinet. Secretary of War Seddon resigned, but in March Davis reaffirmed his faith in Benjamin.[66]

---

[64]John A. Campbell to Hon. R.M.T. Hunter, October 31, 1877, in *Southern Historical Society Papers, Volume IV, July to December 1877* (NC: Broadfoot Publishing Co. [reprint], 1990), 317-318.
[65]Ibid; "Memoranda of the conversation at the conference in Hampton Roads," by John A. Campbell, February 1865, in Pickett Papers, Library of Congress.
[66]Meade, *Benjamin*, 307-309.

"Grateful for the Offer"

Benjamin's career was temporarily salvaged, but the results of a previous operation was quickly unfolding. John H. Surratt of Maryland was sent by Benjamin as a courier to Canada. En route the courier met an acquaintance, actor John Wilkes Booth. Both had spoken earlier of an unofficial abduction of President Lincoln, but Surratt was on official business. Richmond fell to the Union troops, so he advised Booth to give up the plot. On April 4th, 1865, John Surratt boarded a train for New York. Reaching Montreal, he handed the assigned dispatches to General Edward Gray Lee, who led the Confederate operations in Canada in 1865. Edward G. Lee next sent Surratt on a mission. He was to effect the release of Confederate prisoners in Elmira, New York. Surratt was still in the Elmira area when Lincoln was shot at Ford's Theatre in Washington, D.C.[67]

L.Q. and the Confederate State Department was crippled by the time of Lincoln's assassination. In a letter to his half-brother Peter, he outlined his actions at the end of the war. The Confederate Government was in full retreat. They boarded trains and traveled south on the railway to Danville, Virginia. L.Q. went with the fleeing Confederates. He rode on as far as Greensboro, where he heard that General Robert E. Lee had surrendered. On one line, he mentioned he "left for Greensboro or rather Charlotte."[68] This line was telling, for the records of the

---

[67] "A Remarkable Lecture-John H. Surratt Tells His Story," *Lincoln Herald*, December 1949, Volume 51, No. 4, 27-29.
[68] L.Q. Washington to Peter G. Washington, May 5, 1865, Papers of Peter Grayson Washington (MSS 2769), Special Collections Department, University of Virginia Library.

"Grateful for the Offer"

State Department were of great concern to Benjamin; he tasked the remaining clerk, William Bromwell, with the safety of a shipment of the Confederate records to a hiding place in a barn near Charlotte, North Carolina. This completed, L.Q. decided at Greensboro that carrying on as a fugitive was fruitless. The other Confederate officials split up and fled. Davis hoped to reach Confederates in the western states. He was caught in Georgia in early May. Benjamin was luckier and escaped to Europe. Stephens, Seddon, and Hunter were all imprisoned.[69]

L.Q. was more fortunate than many of the other officials. He arrived in Danville on April 14th. Ambling north, he joined a group walking towards the Union lines. About the 25th, they met Union officers and noted their "courtesy" and "civility." After reporting to the provost at Richmond, he wrote Peter Washington that he planned to visit his mother and then search for work in the Virginia capital. He ominously quipped in his letter, "--if the yankees do not hang me."[70]

With his friends imprisoned and no office to hold, L.Q. had no choice but to go home. His life took a turn in the Reconstruction era as a newsman and unofficial representative of Southern interests. His ties to Hunter proved invaluable to the South even

---

[69] L.Q. Washington to President Andrew Johnson, June 28, 1865, M1003, Case Files of Applications from Former Confederates for Presidential Pardons ("Amnesty Papers") 1865-1867, Roll 70, National Archives; Meade, *Benjamin*, 311-312; Ibid., 317-319; Bowman, ed., *Civil War Day by Day,* 214.

[70] Washington to Peter Washington, May 5, 1865, Papers of Peter Grayson Washington (MSS 2769), Special Collections Department, University of Virginia Library.

"Grateful for the Offer"

after the fighting ceased.

Views of Reconstruction from a Southern Correspondent

When the Civil War ended, L.Q. Washington's life was at a crossroads. Political ambition and propinquity to close state secrets faded. However, the crucial months following the surrender of Robert E. Lee's Army of Northern Virginia gave L.Q. a focus. He assisted in the promotion of the cause of the postwar South, especially in obtaining the freedom of an imprisoned Hunter. In doing so, L.Q. made a crucial choice. Remaining in Washington, D.C. meant isolation from any remaining opportunity in Richmond for former Confederate servants. However, his inclination to attempt to personally influence national matters was strong.

L.Q. turned to self-preservation. Hunter was imprisoned at Fort Pulaski, just outside of Savannah, Georgia. Not yet knowing what might be his own peril as a former Confederate official, and having decided upon the best way to assist all concerned, L.Q. did what he had to by returning to Washington, D.C. He petitioned President Andrew Johnson to grant him a pardon. In doing so, L.Q. was unrepentant. He simply stated, "On the 11th of April I heard officially of General Lee's surrender. There was, in my opinion, no longer a possibility of serious resistance to the U.S. armies, save by irregular warfare to which I was opposed..."[1]

With the defeat of the Army of Northern Virginia, L.Q. felt

---

[1] L.Q. Washington to Mrs. R.M.T. Hunter, June 30, 1865, Reel 7, Papers of R.M.T. Hunter Hunter-Garnett Family Papers (MSS 38-45), Special Collections Department, University of Virginia Library; L.Q. Washington to President Andrew Johnson, June 28, 1865, M1003, "Amnesty Papers" 1865-1867, Roll 70, National Archives.

that his obligation to the Confederacy was voided. He took the oath of allegiance to the United States on May 5th, predating the surrender of General Joseph Johnston's North Carolina Confederates by several weeks. The documents went through the military authorities in Washington, D.C. On June 29 the petition went to the Union-appointed Governor of Virginia, Francis H. Pierrepont. The Governor had no objection to the pardon request. To bolster L.Q.'s pardon, Washington mayor Richard Wallach wrote a letter to U.S. Attorney General James Speed stating he knew him well "& sincerely believe that he is honest in his intention."[2] On July 5th, 1865, L.Q. Washington was officially pardoned and returned to Washington city.[3]

A fast pardon for L.Q. did not mean an immediate release for his former comrades. Hunter remained imprisoned at Fort Pulaski for some time. In fact, Hunter corresponded with L.Q., hoping to gain his own freedom through connections. Even Mrs. Hunter wrote L.Q., who attempted to soothe her fears by assuring her of Hunter's continuing health and that he was working furiously for Hunter's release. He wrote Mrs. Hunter on June 30 from Richmond:

> Miss Kate [Campbell] tells me that from her
> father's [Judge John Campbell] letters she infers
> they are all together. She says the place is healthy

---

[2]Washington to Johnson, June 28, 1865, M1003, Roll 70, National Archives; notation on pardon letter from Francis H. Pierrepont, in M1003, National Archives; Richard Wallach to Attorney General James Speed, July 5, 1865, in M1003, National Archives.
[3]Notation on Application of Pardon, no 595, in M1003, National Archives.

& will continue until Sept. & this relieves my anxiety very much. They are tolerably comfortable, by her account & similar accounts, all received from Mr. Seddon.[4]

L.Q. stated he was looking to the services of William Evarts, soon to be a Johnson cabinet member. He wrote Mrs. Hunter that contact was made with Colonel E.W. Hubard, another associate of President Johnson. He reported that Hubard would try to secure Hunter's release.[5] In the meantime, he kept personal contact with Hunter, who began to panic. Hunter wrote on July 7th:

> I hear nothing from Virginia. Why don't you write? I have taken the required oaths and petitioned for amnesty, failing that for leave to return home on parole and failing all these for leave to quit the country. If my friends will exert themselves in behalf of my petition I think they could get me out. Write to some of your friends in Washington. Your brother [half-brother Peter G. Washington] I think would aid me. Write soon.[6]

Hunter had reason to worry. Another of his friends, Louis Crenshaw, feared that Hunter would have to undergo a trial for treason. Governor Pierrepont recommended Hunter's release, but it was uncertain whether a trial would occur. L.Q. reported on July 22nd that Francis Preston Blair made a personal appeal to

---

[4]Washington to Mrs. R.M.T. Hunter, June 30, 1865, Reel 7, Papers of Hunter, Hunter-Garnett Family Papers (MSS 38-45), Special Collections Department, University of Virginia Library.
[5]Ibid.
[6]R.M.T. Hunter to L.Q. Washington, July 7, 1865, Chisholm Papers, Virginia Historical Society.

Views of Reconstruction from a Southern Correspondent

President Johnson to release Hunter and Campbell, but no decision was reached. He stated that Peter Washington had no influence on President Johnson, but that he would be consulted. L.Q. finally suggested that Hunter's personal appeal should be written to Johnson.[7]

> I would suggest that you address a letter to the President asking for the present to be released on parole, with condition to remain at home & report there to the nearest military authorities, and that you enclose this letter in one to Mr. Stanton asking him to endorse & bring the matter before President Johnson. The President has released Govs Brown, Vance, Letcher & Smith in some such terms.[8]

The following day L.Q. saw two judges, Hughes and Denver. Hughes was a congressman from Indiana and a friend of President Johnson. Hughes revealed to L.Q. that the reason Hunter was imprisoned was general fear in Congress that he might inspire others into further opposition, but there was enough political muscle to assure them of the contrary. Although the process had been slow, the combined efforts of his friends finally led to Hunter's release. Hunter was formally paroled September 13, 1865, although Secretary Stanton restricted his freedom heavily in January 1866.[9]

---

[7] L.Q. Washington to R.M.T. Hunter, July 22, 1865, Hunter-Garnett Family Papers (MSS 38-45), Box 34, Special Collections, University of Virginia Library.
[8] Ibid.
[9] L.Q. Washington to R.M.T. Hunter, July 23, 1865, Hunter-Garnett Family Papers (MSS 38-45), Box 34, Special Collections

Views of Reconstruction from a Southern Correspondent

In the wake of Hunter's release, other Confederate leaders asked for some help from L.Q. The former chief clerk of the Confederate War Department, Robert G.H. Kean, turned to him. Kean learned that James A. Seddon was in irons at Pulaski, possibly facing execution from the aftershock of the treatment of war prisoners at Andersonville.

> I sought L.Q. Washington, who was then in Washington, and communicated to him the apprehensions I felt, and urged him to communicate them to Mr. Seddon's friends, with whom I knew him to be intimate. I learned he did so; and Mrs. Seddon sent Captain Phillip Welford, a gentleman of great intelligence, to Washington to see what was best to be done to protect her helpless husband, who was being prosecuted while a prisoner six hundred miles away.[10]

It is a curious twist of fate that L.Q.'s very tendency to serve in the background of national events enabled him to have any sort of success both in aiding his friends and pursuing a new career at all, after the fall of the Confederacy. It seems that L.Q. blended

---

Department, University of Virginia; Simms, *Hunter*, 206.

[10] "Letter of Hon. R.G.H. Kean, Chief Clerk of the Confederate War Department." in *Southern Historical Society Papers, January to June 1876, Volume I* (NC: Broadfoot Books, 1990), 201; Edward Younger, ed., *Inside the Confederate Government-The Diary of Robert Garlick Hill Kean*, Copyright @ 1957 by Oxford University Press, New York, NY, Reprinted by permission of Oxford University Press, 228.

seamlessly back into local society following the war. In fact, many did not know who he was or realized his connection to the fallen Confederacy. Even Kean's diary noted L.Q. only as a newspaper reporter. Shortly after writing Hunter in July, L.Q. went to New York for visits with the Garnett family and Alexander Stephens. In addition, L.Q. arranged to move his mother to new quarters in the District of Columbia. However safely anonymous he was, L.Q. found while seeking gainful employment that politics remained a closed option. Congress disallowed former Confederates to serve in any active political capacity. Many former Confederates bought railroads and business interests to make their fortunes. However, L.Q. did not have the prominence to carry him to that level.[11] He had not been a top political leader in the Confederate Government, nor was he considered a military hero.

He went back to journalism, a field he knew well. Seeking occupational security, L.Q. traveled in the deep South searching for work; however, he spent more time touring the states than actually seeking work. He went overland to Memphis "by way of Bristol." There he boarded a boat on the Mississippi River, stopping at New Orleans and Mobile. Upon leaving the deep

---

[11] Washington to R.M.T. Hunter, September 2, 1865, Papers of Hunter, Hunter-Garnett Family Papers (MSS 38-45), Reel 8, Special Collections, University of Virginia Library; From *The Virginia Conservatives 1867-1879-A Study in Reconstruction Politics* by Jack P. Maddex, Jr. Copyright(c) 1970 by the University of North Carolina Press, 1970. Used by permission of the publisher, 38-39.

Views of Reconstruction from a Southern Correspondent

South, L.Q. headed north to Atlanta and Knoxville before returning to the District of Columbia. He was moved by the decay of war along his sightseeing route. It appeared a greater attraction to L.Q. than prospects of employment there.[12]

> I was absent about a month & after all failed to accomplish the object of a long, tedious and expensive journey. I shall be pleased some day to tell you of my observations. I was profoundly impressed with the mischiefs resulting to labor & industry from military rule. Virginia is, I think, recovering faster than any other state.[13]

On September 1st, L.Q. once again left for White Sulphur Springs, West Virginia, contact with possible employers and the political elite. While at the springs, L.Q. had some luck. He heard that the famous Richmond paper, the *Examiner*, was to be sold. The editor, Garland Pollard, had taken over from John Moncure Daniel upon the latter's death in 1865. He sold the paper to the scholarly Thomas H. Wynne, and from him L.Q. finally received the offer for which he was searching.[14]

> He [Wynne] has asked me in the most flattering & liberal manner to take editorial charge & I have

---

[12] L.Q. Washington to R.M.T. Hunter, January 23, 1866, Papers of Hunter, Hunter-Garnett Family Papers (MSS 38-45), Reel 8, Special Collections Department, University of Virginia Library.
[13] Ibid.
[14] L.Q. Washington to R.M.T. Hunter, September 23, 1866, Papers of Hunter, Hunter-Garnett Family Papers (MSS 38-45), Reel 8, Special Collections Department, University of Virginia Library.

agreed to do so though my business prospects in Washington had greatly improved in the last two months. The transfer is not announced nor my connection as Editor...[15]

The business of journalism in postwar Virginia was painstaking and transitory. Pollard left the *Examiner* to the new ownership, and L.Q. complained that the transition made him want to leave Richmond. Nonetheless, he believed the paper was still strong enough to survive bad circulation. Abruptly changing his mind, L.Q. officially took his position as editor of the *Examiner* on September 27, 1866. He tried to maintain a continuous readership by liberal subscription terms. In November he wrote defaulted subscriber William R. Aylett of King William County that he and Wynne had revised a distribution list of the paper. They allowed Aylett to continue to receive the paper until "your means or some change in our arrangements shall make it proper to be otherwise regulated."[16]

---

[15]Ibid.
[16]Washington to Hunter, September 23, 1866, Papers of Hunter, Hunter-Garnett Family Papers (MSS 38-45), Special Collections Department, University of Virginia Library; L.Q. Washington to R.M.T. Hunter, November 17, 1866, Papers of Hunter, Hunter-Garnett Family Papers (MSS 38-45), Special Collections Department, University of Virginia Library, Reel 8; L.Q.Washington to William R. Aylett, November 5, 1866, in Aylett Family Papers, Virginia Historical Society. Thomas Hicks Wynne (1820-1875) was involved in newspapers shortly after the death of John Moncure Daniel the previous year. He went to other pursuits after 1869. See William Ernst, "Thomas Hicks Wynne-Horatio Alger in Nineteenth-Century Richmond," *Virginia*

Views of Reconstruction from a Southern Correspondent

Despite efforts at the *Examiner*, the personal victory of attaining editorship did not mean permanent occupational security. The paper experienced drawbacks in content and business practices. In doing so, L.Q. blamed previous editors for their lack of input. In December he made a quick visit home but, "chained" to the paper, he returned to Richmond before Christmas. Shortly thereafter, L.Q. received word that Wynne sold two-thirds of his interest in the *Examiner* to A.M. Keily of Petersburg. This signaled the end of L.Q.'s brief time at the helm of the paper. Keily wanted personal creative control as majority owner. In early January, L.Q. wrote Hunter that he was "thrown out."[17]

L.Q.'s fortunes continued to decline. He remarked that the "*Bulletin* (of Memphis) preferred Com. Rafael Semmes (of the Alabama) to me." L.Q. hoped that Dick Smith of the other major Richmond newspaper, the *Enquirer*, wanted to sell his paper due to a pending appointment. However, the *Enquirer* merged with the floundering *Examiner*. A five man board appointed a young

---

Cavalcade, Volume 27, No. 4, Spring 1978.
[17]L.Q. Washington to R.M.T. Hunter, December 11, 1866, Papers of Hunter, Hunter-Garnett Family Papers (MSS 38-45), Special Collections Department, University of Virginia Library, Reel 8; L.Q. Washington to R.M.T. Hunter, December 20, 1866, Papers of Hunter, Hunter-Garnett Family Papers (MSS 38-45), Special Collections Department, University of Virginia Library, Reel 8; L.Q. Washington to R.M.T. Hunter, January 2, 1867, Papers of Hunter, Hunter-Garnett Family Papers (MSS 38-45), Special Collections Department, University of Virginia Library, Reel 8.

editor out of Danville, William D. Coleman. Although L.Q. held down minimal work as a correspondent with the *London Telegraph*, an editor's position eluded him.[18]

While he struggled in his endeavors to find employment, Governor Pierrepont and President Andrew Johnson tried to reunite the North and South by conservative tactics. By 1866, Johnson was attacked by critics in Congress largely under the leadership of Pennsylvanian Thaddeus Stevens.[19] Truly concerned over the bleak prospects of moderate measures, L.Q. wrote bitterly to friends. To one he wrote, "I find a bad state of things here [Washington, D.C.] All our friends are greatly depressed & ready to up...the President is said to be thoroughly cowed..the impression is that he will be impeached if it is essential to the Radical plans..."[20]

---

[18] L.Q. Washington to R.M.T. Hunter, March 21, 1867, Papers of Hunter, Hunter-Garnett Family Papers (MSS 38-45), Special Collections Department, University of Virginia Library, Reel 8; L.Q. Washington to R.M.T. Hunter, April 21, 1867, Papers of Hunter, Hunter-Garnett Family Papers, Special Collections, University of Virginia Library, Reel 8; L.Q. Washington to R.M.T. Hunter, July 19, 1867, Papers of Hunter, Hunter-Garnett Family Papers, Special Collections, University of Virginia Library, Reel 8.

[19] From *The Virginia Conservatives* by Jack P. Maddex, Jr., Used by permission of the publisher, 41; Richard Lowe, *Republicans and Reconstruction in Virginia, 1856-70* (Charlottesville, VA: University Press of Virginia, 1991), 90-92.

[20] L.Q. Washington to R.H. Maury Esq., February 12, 1867, Brock Collection, Box 112. This item is reproduced by permission of The Huntington Library, San Marino, California.

Views of Reconstruction from a Southern Correspondent

Virginia's moderate government slipped away in the summer of 1867, with the assumption of control by a radical wing of the Republican Party. By splitting up the moderates at a convention in Richmond, any conservative movement was crushed.[21] From the Capitol's vantage point, L.Q. forecast this in a letter to his friend Robert Alexander of Richmond in March 1867, hastily writing Alexander that he had sent word to a contact at the *Richmond Enquirer* that Virginians had no choice but organize else be disenfranchised.[22]

> My interviews here is with the ablest & most prominent of Northern Conservatives & I also see much of the newspaper men, the Southerners who come here & some thing of the Radical Congressmen. I would not have written this letter if I did not feel how much depended on the course Virginia may now take. The position of the South is very critical. We are the most helpless people on God's earth & I look in vain for allies...[23]

Still L.Q. held out hope of a "conservative reaction" in the northern states, but he acknowledged that "its evidence are not yet sufficiently striking notorious to impress..."[24] He based this "sentiment" on county elections in West Virginia where several

---

[21] Lowe, *Republicans and Reconstruction in Virginia*, 90-92.
[22] Washington to Robert Alexander Lancaster, Esq., March 9, 1867, in Lancaster Family Papers, Virginia Historical Society.
[23] Ibid.
[24] L.Q. Washington to R.H. Maury Esq., April 21, 1867, Brock Collection, Box 112. This item is reproduced by permission of the Huntington Library, San Marino, California.

"radical" candidates were defeated.[25]

Summer brought a welcome break from covering events in Washington regarding Virginia's suffrage issue, but this hardly kept L.Q. from seeking new opportunities to promote former Confederates. In August L.Q. found himself among the Lees at Sweet Springs, West Virginia. Having spoken again to Custis Lee, L.Q. broached the idea that the elder Lee consider the presidency of the Chesapeake & Ohio Railroad Company. It would allow the old general "a wider sphere of usefulness than his present duties [at Washington College] & enable him to move about more..."[26] Custis Lee felt his father refused to impair careers of any other individual to gain the position, but promised to speak to him about it. As was common with visits to the Virginia spas, most of the party reconvened at White Sulphur Springs within days. No further correspondence apparently survived on the issue, but Lee was satisfied with his position at Washington College and remained there until his death.[27]

The December Constitutional Convention of Virginia was loaded with more radical elements. Many of the representatives were newcomers arriving from the north, or "carpetbaggers."

---

[25] L.Q. Washington to R.H. Maury, June 8, 1867, Brock Collection, Box 112. This item is reproduced by permission of the Huntington Library, San Marino, California.

[26] L.Q. Washington to R.H. Maury, August 22, 1867, Brock Collection, Box 112. This item is reproduced by permission of the Huntington Library, San Marino, California.

[27] Ibid.

Views of Reconstruction from a Southern Correspondent

The Underwood Convention, as it was called, was bitterness to most Virginians. Although not representative of the state, many of the moderate elements rallied around Robert M.T. Hunter. They founded the Conservative Party in November 1867 from the foundations of individual state committees comprising old line Whigs and former Constitutional Unionists from previous elections. L.Q. hailed the formation as a spirited gathering reminiscent of old Virginia.[28]

L.Q. was a spectator during this period. Although he obtained employment from the late W.W. Seaton's *National Intelligencer* in 1868, he did not involve himself in politics. Unfortunately the newspaper was on a downward spiral after Seaton's death two years earlier. Its longtime position as a political organ was endangered by newer papers.[29]

As reflected in the fate of the *Intelligencer*, things looked bleak for Virginia in early 1868. The conservatives rallied early, hoping to stop the downward turn of events. They prepared an official address to Congress asking for the readmission of Virginia. The Committee was under the leadership of Alexander H.H. Stuart.[30] L.Q. returned from Richmond in late January. He

---

[28]Lowe, *Republicans and Reconstruction*,129-131; From the *Virginia Conservatives* by Jack P. Maddex, Jr., 55-56. Used by permission of the publisher.
[29]Raymond H. Pulley, *Old Virginia Restored-An Interpretation of the Progressive Impulse, 1870-1930* (Charlottesville: University Press of Virginia, 1968), 10; From the *Virginia Conservatives* by Jack P. Maddex, Jr., 37. Used by permission of the publisher.
[30]From the *Virginia Conservatives* by Jack P. Maddex, Jr., 68.

wrote Hunter he was "gratified to hear that you [Hunter] are to prepare the address. The point is to impress Northern sentiment and I think that you can do this more skilfully [sic] than the others."[31] L.Q. cautioned that it was preferable to have Thomas Stanley Bocock of Buckingham County, a man with a good deal of legislative experience, to assist in the process of drafting the address. Instead, Stuart appointed William C. MacFarland, who in turn gave Hunter the job.[32]

As the official draft of the address was in process to reassure Virginia's right to the suffrage, L.Q. was involved in another extraordinary plan to influence the coming national elections, assisting Virginia Democrat John Randolph Tucker in swaying opinion on Capitol Hill by gathering statistical information. He named General Francis Preston Blair, Jr. as a possible presidential candidate as early as February 1868, warning Hunter that it was a "danger to be guarded against...going for the man we would prefer instead of the man we can elect."[33] An alliance with the Blair family was not surprising as they had recently defected

---

[31]Washington to Hunter, February 17, 1868, Papers of Hunter, Hunter-Garnett Family Papers (MSS 38-45), Special Collections Department, University of Virginia Library, Reel 9.
[32]Ibid.; Thomas Cary Johnson, *The Hon. Thomas Bocock* (Lynchburg, VA: JP Bell, undated), 3; From *Virginia Conservatives* by Jack P. Maddex, Jr., 56. Used by Permission. Bocock (1815-91) was a leading Democratic figure in Virginia politics.
[33]Washington to Hunter, February 17, 1868, Papers of Hunter, Hunter-Garnett Family Papers (MSS 38-45), Special Collections Department, University of Virginia Library, Reel 9.

Views of Reconstruction from a Southern Correspondent

from their existing ties with the Republican Party as the radicals displaced their access to power. The party of Lincoln and Johnson reforms was gone and with it the influence of the Blair family. L.Q. and Tucker found formidable political allies to readmit Virginia in the Union.[34]

It was at this time that L.Q. felt the financial pinch of Reconstruction. Although he actively wrote for the *National Intelligencer*, a job which began at the beginning of that year, he complained he received

> ...a meagre compensation for amount and quality of work done that my articles receive at least as much credit as they deserve & I think I stand well with the Proprietors & Editors. This came in good season, the year 1867 having been the most embarrassing in my whole life & last week I could not go to a party at [John H.] Coyle's because I had no clothes fit to go in.[35]

---

[34] William Ernest Smith, *The Francis Preston Blair Family in Politics, Volume II* (New York, NY: Da Capo Press, 1969), 401; From the *Virginia Conservative* by Jack P. Maddex, Jr., 65. Used by permission.

[35] Washington to Hunter, February 17, 1868, Papers of Hunter, Hunter-Garnett Family Papers (MSS 38-45), Special Collections Department, University of Virginia Library, Reel 9. John H. Coyle was the owner of the *National Intelligencer*. The Intelligencer was still very active in Democratic politics, often mirroring Manton Marble's *New York World*. George McJimsey, *Genteel Partisan: Manton Marble, 1834-1917* (Ames, IA: The Iowa State Press, 1971), 128-129.

Despite the financial shortcomings, L.Q. felt his work with the *Intelligencer* to be vital. In his continual quest for allies in the Capital City, he found "the *National Intelligencer* has more able thinkers who write for it, than any other paper but it does not give news or public documents with the fulness [sic] of the *[New York] World* or *Herald*."[36] To James Lyons in Richmond, he wrote, "...I think its [the *Intelligencer*] editorials have been fuller & abler than any journal North of the Potomac in opposing & unmasking Radicalism."[37]

In early April, L.Q. received critical praise for his journalistic work. He wrote Hunter that his pieces for the *Intelligencer* "proved to suit the public taste & have gained me an unexpected & quite flattering degree of reputation."[38] He had an editorial series called "Notes at the Capitol," which got good exposure in the spring of 1868. L.Q. furthered his contacts with Northern newsmen, such as the *Boston Globe's* Ben Purley Poore.[39] The contact with newsmen were not always on friendly terms; L.Q. wrote to Lyons about a row with another journalist at Willard's Hotel.

---

[36]Ibid.
[37]L.Q. Washington to Hon. James Lyons, March 20, 1868, Brock Collection, This item is reproduced by permission of the Huntington Library, San Marino, California.
[38]Washington to Hunter, April 7, 1868, Papers of Hunter, Hunter-Garnett Family Papers (MSS 38-45), Special Collections Department, University of Virginia Library, Reel 9.
[39]Ibid.

Views of Reconstruction from a Southern Correspondent

>As to the row, I was insulted in the Senate gallery by a Radical correspondent named Painter--I had done or said nothing to provoke his malignity but I suppose he knew I was a southerner. I did not notice his insolence there but met him at Willard's & after trying to induce him to go <u>outside</u>, slapped his face there which led to a very small fight without results save the immediate interference on which he counted in both places. Such is our Civilization. God help us.[40]

The national election conventions were vital to the question of Virginia's suffrage. The Republicans nominated General Ulysses S. Grant. L.Q. immediately suggested to Hunter that another military man of high reputation be nominated by the Democrats. Winfield Scott Hancock, one of the heroes of Gettysburg, was his suggested nominee. He pleaded that the "South has everything at stake & cannot afford to lose the election, or finesse for preferences."[41]

Hope appeared in Virginia, but it was quickly dashed. The results of the Underwood Convention revealed the worst. Former Confederates were barred from office. Many were effectively disenfranchised unless they passed a "test oath." This entailed an "ironclad" pact with the Union. The military occupancy troops under Union General John Schofield found the radical presence in the state to be too heavy-handed and did much to temper some

---

[40] Washington to Lyons, March 20, 1868, Brock Collection, This item is reproduced by permission of the Huntington Library, San Marino, California.
[41] Ibid.

of the articles, including the office and "test oath" provisions. Conservatives were in an uproar over the presence of Union General Benjamin Butler, who had gained the nickname of "Beast" for his harsh treatment of Southern ladies during the war, and the Ku Klux Klan made its first appearances in Virginia during the convention. The convention was delayed over processes, and lost much of its effectiveness; by mid-April it disbanded.[42]

L.Q. was unable to leave Washington during the Underwood Convention. Instead he concentrated on the upcoming Democratic Convention. He wrote to Hunter on June 21st that "Congress has given us all a good deal of trouble & me particularly. I have had to watch them & have done a very large amount of work for the *Intelligencer*."[43] He maintained that a [Presidential] movement nominating Supreme Court Justice Salmon P. Chase was doomed to fail and he blamed the "tricksters" (mainly New York politicians) for advancing him as, "...the best man for our people, is Frank P. Blair. He says the Reconstruction laws must be stamped out & talks bolder & more emphatic than any of the Candidates."[44] L.Q. wrote that he was

---

[42]From the *Virginia Conservatives* by Jack P. Maddex, Jr., 59; Ibid., 63; Lowe, *Republicans and Reconstruction in Virginia*, 140-141.
[43]Washington to Hunter, June 21, 1868. Papers of Hunter, Hunter-Garnett Family Papers (MSS 38-45), Special Collections Department, University of Virginia Library, Reel 9.
[44]McJimsey, *Genteel Partisan*, 126-127; Washington to Hunter, June 21, 1868, Papers of Hunter, Hunter-Garnett Family Papers

to go to New York for the Democratic Convention. Highlighting his mission, he stated, "We are <u>threatened</u> with a bill to cut off additional registration in Va. That would cost us 15,000 votes. Another danger is fraud in counting votes."[45]

In July, L.Q. traveled to New York for the convention. There he met sympathetic colleagues Robert Barnwell Rhett, Jr. of South Carolina, Thomas Clingman of North Carolina, and J.W. Stevenson of Kentucky. He visited John B. Gordon and Nathan Bedford Forrest. L.Q. reported that the New York delegation was against Southern and Western interests. The South won on some Democratic platform issues, but the candidacy was in a quandary. The South would not support Chase; however their favored candidates, Hancock and Pendleton, could not succeed either. By the end of the convention, New Yorker Horatio Seymour emerged as the candidate, as he appeared acceptable to both sections. Frank Blair's name was sent out as a candidate for Vice-President. L.Q. was satisfied with the results.[46]

L.Q. and Tucker met secretly with Frank Blair's brother and former U.S. Postmaster General Montgomery Blair. A plan was devised between the three. They would hold a "shadow" vote in

---

(MSS 38-45), Special Collections, University of Virginia Library, Reel 9.

[45]Washington to Hunter, June 21, 1868, Papers of Hunter, Hunter-Garnett Family Papers (MSS 38-45), Special Collections, University of Virginia Library, Reel 9.

[46]Washington to Hunter, August 2, 1868, Papers of Hunter, Hunter-Garnett Family Papers (MSS 38-45), Special Collections Department, University of Virginia Library, Reel 9.

Views of Reconstruction from a Southern Correspondent

Virginia for the Presidency. The hope was that it would influence the vote indirectly. With the repercussions of the Underwood Convention, the three thought it necessary. L.Q. planned a lot of positive press for Blair's brother. With no real committee to represent Democrats in Virginia, L.Q. pointed to an obscure section of the state code that allowed "any two freeholders present" to act as representatives. He argued that a convention was not necessary to confirm their legitimacy. However, it never got past the planning stages when moderates made gains. Although never tried, it was hoped that Seymour and Blair could achieve a victory over Grant in the fall. The results might reverse the direction of radical sentiment towards Virginia.[47]

The convention ended on a hopeful note. L.Q., who stayed in New York afterwards, was tired. He wrote Hunter, "After 7 months of good work I am going to the White Sulphur of Greenbrier, West Va to recruit my forces for fall work."[48] He mentioned his work was tri-fold. In August 1868 he was an associate editor for the *National Intelligencer*, recently attained. In addition, he was a correspondent for the *London Telegraph* and the *Cincinnati Enquirer*. With all the duties at these three

---

[47] From the *Virginia Conservatives* by Jack P. Maddex, Jr., 65. Used by Permission; L.Q. Washington to John Randolph Tucker, July 31, 1868, Tucker Family Papers, Southern Historical Collection, Wilson Library, University of North Carolina at Chapel Hill.

[48] Washington to Hunter, August 2, 1868, Papers of Hunter, Hunter-Garnett Family Papers (MSS 38-45), Special Collections Department, University of Virginia Library, Reel 9.

Views of Reconstruction from a Southern Correspondent

posts and additional political work, there was little wonder he was fatigued.[49]

The rest at White Sulphur signaled the end of much of L.Q.'s political work that year. The "shadow" campaign tactics of Tucker and Blair ended suddenly when Republicans made gains within the state under a new Governor, Henry Wells. After grappling with radicals for a time, Wells moderated the party direction by eliminating some radicals from state offices. He was able to gather some prominent Virginians, such as former Confederate cavalry general Williams C. Wickham, to support Grant in Richmond. The North was decisively for Grant, and a Democratic victory looked unlikely in early fall.[50]

As L.Q. returned to Washington in late September, he noticed the political shift. Equally distressing to him was the immoderate views of traditionalists in Virginia. From his vantage point, L.Q. felt the state was best served with a moderate stance. This was a notable shift from his prewar thinking and more towards Hunter's own view. The best way to free the state from Reconstruction policy was to parley with the North and not offend them. However, L.Q. was sanguine about the situation. He wrote,

---

[49] Ibid.
[50] From the *Virginia Conservatives* by Jack P. Maddex, Jr., 65. Used by Permission; Lowe, *Republicans and Reconstruction in Virginia*, 156-157; Washington to Hunter, September 25, 1868, Papers of Hunter, Hunter-Garnett Family Papers (MSS 38-45), Special Collections Department, University of Virginia Library, Reel 9.

Views of Reconstruction from a Southern Correspondent

"Indeed, I fear that Grant will be elected. The speeches of Wade Hampton, Bowie & others have been used to inflame the Northern mind against us & with signal effect."[51]

Grant was favored to win, yet L.Q. wrote there remained hope for Seymour in September. A Democratic hold on Pennsylvania and Indiana were needed as two crucial Northern bases of support. As there was a strong link between Grant and the Radicals in Congress, L.Q. gave little hope for Virginia if Seymour lost. As if he knew the outcome, Washington offered an olive branch when he wrote, "Personally I think Grant a better man than Johnson & certainly at the close of the war, his temper was better."[52]

The expected election results came, but good fortune assisted Virginia in overcoming military Reconstruction. Governor Wells made enemies of crucial supporters such as William Mahone. A group of moderates under Alexander Stuart took the advantage of ridding themselves of the Underwood Constitution's two hardest articles, the "test oath" and office provision. Stuart decided to ask Congress for full voting rights and amnesty for all state citizens, which included African-Americans. However, L.Q. had taken a rare step from the background to an extraverted position. He wrote President Andrew Johnson on the 17th of December,

---

[51]Washington to Hunter, September 25, 1868, Papers of Hunter, Hunter-Garnett Family Papers (MSS 38-45), Special Collections Department, University of Virginia Library, Reel 9.
[52]Ibid.

Views of Reconstruction from a Southern Correspondent

asking for full amnesty as a Christmas proclamation.[53]

> Will you allow me to offer for your consideration the propriety of selecting next Christmas Day for an unconditional amnesty of all persons participating in the recent rebellion, naming no individual, and excepting none whether by name, or class, or description of any sort. I have thought much of it and I am within bounds in saying that this step would be cordially approved by a large majority of the American people, <u>acceptable</u> to, at least, two thirds of them, and in Europe would be hailed by all as a graceful, humane and statesman-like act. I have always believed that you did not intend to close your Presidential term without such an act, and I sincerely trust for the sake of the country and your own fame that you will not allow this, the fittest occasion, for a general amnesty to pass.[54]

L.Q. wanted Johnson to close the door on Reconstruction before the end of his term. However, L.Q.'s plea was the only one to reach Johnson, and the President was worn down from his frequent fights and near impeachment at the hands of Congress. The next request for amnesty would have to be submitted to their President-Elect Grant. In order to formalize efforts for political equality and amnesty, Conservatives formed a group to draft the

---

[53]From the *Virginia Conservatives* by Jack P. Maddex, Jr., 66-69. Used by Permission; L.Q. Washington to President Andrew Johnson, December 17, 1868, Andrew Johnson Papers, Reel 35, Manuscripts Division, Library of Congress.
[54]Washington to Johnson, December 17, 1868, Reel 9, Library of Congress.

goals of Virginia's political future.[55]

In early 1869 the Conservatives emerged stronger. The Stuart group, drawn from moderate Democrats and former Whigs in Virginia, known as the "Committee of Nine," began critical work in January. L.Q. remained in the background, but assisted the Committee in publicity matters. Internal strife remained within the state government, but L.Q. advised Hunter against rash action. He was concerned about carpetbaggers and the split of the moderate and radical wings of the Republican Party. Such a split might cause further instability for the state. A Mahone ally, Gilbert C. Walker, was elected Governor of Virginia in July.[56]

Walker's victory meant that careful construction of a plan to readmit Virginia into the Union was underway. Walker did away with the radical elements and allied with moderates to anchor his own power. Virginia was readmitted to the Union on January 26, 1870. While Reconstruction loomed and increased in intensity in other states, the moderate Conservatives and their good relations with the military authorities saw the process end there. However, L.Q. was far from finished with politics. With the state order restored, opportunities opened.[57]

---

[55]Ibid.; From the *Virginia Conservatives* by Jack P. Maddex, Jr., 69. Used by Permission.
[56]From the *Virginia Conservatives* by Jack P. Maddex, Jr., 69-74. Used by permission; Ibid., 76.
[57]Lowe, *Republicans and Reconstruction in Virginia*, 180-181; Ibid., 50n.

Editorial Wars, Greenbacks, and Redemption

At the beginning of 1870, Littleton Quinton Washington was a committed news correspondent. He was listed as one of the official press members at the Capitol in a directory that year. His home was listed at 1000 6th Street, which was likely one of several lots owned by his brother-in-law Doctor Warwick Evans. L.Q. retained a strong interest in politics at both state and national levels. Reconstruction was over for Virginians, but there remained a struggle for financial stability.

L.Q. was also concerned about finances and his work status reflected this. He knew the difficult economic nature of print concerns, and that even newspapers as solid as the *National Intelligencer* might not last beyond a finite period. Having been employed by several failed newspapers, there was reason for discomfort. It was to be a most challenging period in the seasoned newsman's life.[1] L.Q. wrote for short stretches with the *Petersburg Index* in addition to his piecemeal correspondence work for the *London Telegraph* and the *New York World*. He complained to Hunter in a March 1870 letter that "all my time is engrossed-This is a low sort of work as respects quality. The whole gives me a meager living owing to the high prices of every thing here [in Washington, D.C.]."[2]

As if a tonic from financial woes, he remained focused on state politics. L.Q. stated that he had visited Richmond in the

---

[1] J. Harry Shannon, "Rambler's Explorations Lead Him to Several Literary Circles," *The Washington Star Sunday Magazine*, February 20, 1927, Vol. 2, no. 136.
[2] L.Q. Washington to Hunter, March 9, 1870, Papers of Hunter, Hunter-Garnett Family Papers (MSS 38-45), Special Collections Department, University of Virginia Library, Reel 10.

beginning of March 1870, concerned over the state of Virginia politics. However, the talk changed from state survival to business interests. He questioned the ambitions and the rising career in the Virginia Democratic party of businessman John Strode Barbour. He was a near relation to former Virginia Governor and U.S. Secretary of State James Barbour. John Barbour served as president of several railroads, including the Orange & Alexandria and the Virginia Midland. L.Q. found that Barbour was also in the newspaper publishing business. In his capacity as correspondent, L.Q. felt the editor's business acumen superceded quality print material.[3]

> I saw Barbour but did not have any business intercourse with him. I mean that I have no connection with his paper. I like him very well but I do not trust him wholly. I fear he will be selfish in his paper-pursuing the ends of the Balto & Ohio R.R.-his own ambition. Despite his general ability he is not qualified I think to edit a newspaper. That is a profession in itself & mere editorial discussion will not do to raise a paper.[4]

The same letter to Hunter indicated that L.Q. still sought a solid position within the publishing trade such as the one he enjoyed briefly with the *Intelligencer*. He took interest in a new publishing venture in his hometown.

---

[3]Ibid.; Allen W. Moger, *Virginia-Bourbonism to Byrd, 1870-1925* (Charlottesville, VA: The University Press of Virginia, 1968), 99.
[4]Washington to Hunter, March 9, 1870, Papers of Hunter, Hunter-Garnett Family Papers, Special Collections Department, University of Virginia Library, Reel 10.

Editorial Wars, Greenbacks, and Redemption

> I am much dissatisfied with the newspaper business as respects profits & especially with the nature of my present engagements. [James G.] Barret is trying to get up a paper here [Washington, D.C.] & says he will raise the money. He will make Jas. E. Harvey Editor & I am not sure that I would be offered a subordinate place on the paper, though I would probably have the tender of a place at small & inadequate compensation.[5]

James G. Barret and James E. Harvey were politicians as much as career newspaper correspondents. Barret served as Mayor of Washington and Harvey in a European diplomatic post. The proposed paper had prestigious backers such as banker George W. Riggs and William W. Corcoran. There was a question of reputation, as any new paper needed stature to gain solvency. However, L.Q. hesitated to accept an inadequate position which compromised his current earnings.[6]

According to his correspondence, some things in L.Q.'s life remained stable. His friendships with most Virginians stayed strong. He remained a friend and supporter to his friend Robert M.T. Hunter and wrote him frequently as in prior years. He drew closer to Frank Gildart Ruffin, a newspaper man in Richmond. As always, he kept in contact with Richmond politicians and

---

[5] Ibid.
[6] James H. Whyte, *The Uncivil War-Washington During the Reconstruction, 1865-1878* (New York: Twayne Publishers, 1958), 98; Washington to Hunter, March 9, 1870, Papers of Hunter, Hunter-Garnett Family Papers (MSS 38-45), Special Collections Department, University of Virginia Library, Reel 10.

remained an important link with affairs in the North.[7]

L.Q. became a catalyst to Hunter's desire to write his account of the late war, particularly the Hampton Roads Conference in 1865. Hunter had lost much of his wealth and was forced to sell his lands in the other parts of the state. Several other major Confederate figures were then writing their accounts, particularly Jefferson Davis. In order to publish his own recollections of crucial war accounts, Hunter turned to L.Q.'s contacts in the publishing business. L.Q. asked James Harvey and Manton Marble, the editor of the *The World,* of the possibilities of interested presses in Philadelphia. He also suggested that Hunter write former Confederate John Esten Cooke for assistance; Cooke was by this time an accomplished writer.[8]

L.Q. knew little about the business of book publication, and suggested articles as an alternative. By presenting his views in such a fashion, L.Q. believed, Hunter could send it to *Galaxy,* a leading magazine of the time, or *The World* as a newspaper exclusive. L.Q. thought *Galaxy* would publish an article on the Hampton Roads Conference as it would be an exclusive. The conference was not well canvassed by previous accounts.[9]

In late April L.Q. was feeling the financial pinch himself, remarking to Hunter that he would like to "be under my own

---

[7]Washington to Hunter, March 9, 1870, Papers of Hunter, Hunter-Garnett Family Papers (MSS 38-45), Special Collections Department, University of Virginia Library, Reel 10.
[8]L.Q. Washington to R.M.T. Hunter, April 24, 1870, Papers of Hunter, Garnett-Hunter Family Papers (MSS 38-45), Special Collections Department, University of Virginia Library, Reel 10.
[9]Ibid.

roof."¹⁰ The correspondent complained that his earnings were not enough. He was angry at Barret and Harvey for being "jealous & hostile." They balked at hiring him. He picked up new work from the Kentucky Democratic paper, the *Louisville Ledger*. While achieving this and retaining work with the *London Telegraph*, the money was not enough.¹¹

L.Q. wrote to Hunter on July 18th and mentioned the forthcoming Democratic paper in Washington. He stated that Harvey was the editor, but there was the possibility of writing for the new paper. L.Q. prided himself on his journalistic reputation. With the lack of creative control under Harvey, he missed the days of the *Intelligencer*.¹²

Despite unhappy circumstances in work and finances, L.Q. left for White Sulphur Springs in early August. He expected the arrival of old friends like General James and Mary Chesnut, James M. Mason, and others. The subject of new writings on the Confederacy resurfaced during their conversations, as L.Q. heard that Alexander Stephens' account was released to the public. There was sharp disagreement over Stephens' view of the 1864 Peace Movement. Stephens' view caused a stir among former Confederates, particularly Davis and Mason. Mason was interested in Hunters view of the Peace Movement, which viewed the process less critically of his fellow ex-Confederates. While he was resting in the West Virginia mountains, L.Q. became

---

¹⁰Ibid.
¹¹Ibid.
¹²Ibid.

literary agent for Hunter's forthcoming project.[13]

L.Q. decided to combine his role as Hunter's agent with job seeking. He returned to his hometown on September 7th and prepared for a visit to New York City. He temporarily corresponded for the *Daily Telegraph* during his visit. Hunter was interested in having the well-known publishers in the Appleton family consider his work. L.Q. visited the publishing hub of Grand Street on Hunter's behalf shortly after his arrival. He confessed that he knew little on the subject of book contracts, so he suggested that Hunter get advice from Virginians living in New York. On his personal job prospects, L.Q. was less inspired, even hard on himself. He wrote Hunter, "...I feel like an old man. My life is a failure. Luck is against me. Still I shall struggle on & do my best."[14]

The working vacation to New York did not overcome his political interests. L.Q. was upset by the apparent support of his friend Lewis Harvie to nominate Robert Ould to the Senate. Ould, another ex-Confederate office holder and a district attorney, was L.Q.'s admitted "personal enemy." This likely stemmed from competition in their common youth in Washington, where both previously resided. During the war, Ould presided over the exchange of prisoners.[15]

---

[13]Ibid.; L.Q. Washington to R.M.T. Hunter, September 8, 1870, Papers of Hunter, Hunter-Garnett Family Papers (MSS 38-45), Special Collections Department, University of Virginia Library, Reel 10.
[14]Ibid.
[15]Ibid.; Ould (1820-1881) was serving as an attorney in Richmond.

Editorial Wars, Greenbacks, and Redemption

L.Q. reported to Hunter on October 25th that he had presented the Appletons with his query letter. It was the publisher's policy to avoid decisions on publication until the entire work was reviewed. He met with University Publishing, who considered publication of Hunter's account. Moderate success was attained with Charles Scribner. L.Q. had a friend working in the company, who introduced L.Q. to Scribner himself. He wrote, "Mr. S-- heard me patiently, made no objection, did not commit himself & we agreed that I should on coming back put in writing the scheme of work &c."[16]

Upon leaving New York, L.Q. planned a visit to Richmond. He asked Hunter to meet him. He planned his stay near Linden Row at the home of Dr. Peebles on Franklin Street. As fate would have it, L.Q. spent two weeks in Richmond without seeing Hunter. Instead of working with Hunter on the statesman's political future, he saw friends like Jefferson Davis, James Seddon, and Lewis Harvie during this time. It is unclear why Hunter declined the visit.[17]

November saw the appearance of the new Washington D.C. Democratic paper, the *Daily Patriot*. As predicted, James E. Harvey became editor. Obviously disappointed with the choice, L.Q. criticized the decision with the words that Harvey was "the

---

[16] L.Q. Washington to R.M.T. Hunter, October 25, 1870, in Papers of Hunter, Hunter-Garnett Family Papers (MSS 38-45), Special Collections Department, University of Virginia Library, Reel 10.
[17] Ibid.; L.Q. Washington to R.M.T. Hunter, November 29, 1870, in Papers of Hunter, Hunter-Garnett Family Papers (MSS 38-45), Special Collections Department, University of Virginia Library, Reel 10.

most cranky, critical & disagreeable man I ever had to deal with."[18] He was further disappointed by the rigid content control of New York stockholders in the paper and a thirty dollar a week salary. He suspected the Democratic machine center in New York, Tammany Hall, might have undue influence. L.Q. expected a short stay with the paper.[19]

L.Q.'s increased anxiety over all aspects of the paper affected his health. He fell ill in Virginia in December and was forced to bed for two weeks. Although not sure what ailed him, he suspected typhoid fever. L.Q. characteristically criticized his doctor's demeanor, noting he did not ask detailed questions of the patient's symptoms. Fearful of further decline, he traveled to the warmer climate of Florida and South Carolina.[20]

L.Q. believed national political events favored Southern Democrats. The "Reform Republicans," or moderates, turned against the re-election of Grant. The President was surrounded by scandals in his inner circle. L.Q. was impressed that the reformers within the Republican Party turned against corrupt elements. He spoke well of Carl Schurz as "the master spirit & tactician of the movement."[21] L.Q. felt that both Senators Henry Wilson and Charles Sumner disliked the scandals around Grant, but lacked the courage for an open breach. As a result, Grant's status as the Republican nominee for the 1872 election seemed

---

[18]Ibid.
[19]Ibid.
[20]L.Q. Washington to R.M.T. Hunter, January 6, 1871, in Papers of Hunter, Hunter-Garnett Family Papers (MSS 38-45), Special Collections Department, University of Virginia Library, Reel 10.
[21]Ibid.

certain.²²

While in his sickbed, L.Q. received a letter from Charles Scribner regarding Hunter's publication request. Scribner felt a book of Hunter's reminiscences of the late war would best sell by individual advance order, known as subscription. Daunted by this option, L.Q. wrote to Hunter to consider consulting the Philadelphia-based National Publishing Company, which handled Alexander Stephens' book.²³

By February 1871 L.Q. was increasingly pessimistic about the operations at the *Patriot*. His personal loathing for its two powerful leaders, Barret and Harvey, hardened. While the two politically-connected men handled creative control, L.Q.'s feeling resulted from their powerful ties. He felt his reputable work warranted a more prestigious position on the *Patriot*. To L.Q., the thirty dollar a week salary was insulting. However, friends advised him to exercise due patience to achieve eventual awards. Instead there came a different result.²⁴

> I never had a more odious man to deal with than Harvey. We got on badly until finally about Christmas. I came to an open rupture-Barret playing a double part, but really <u>acting</u> with Harvey. Of course, if the paper were in good hands a position as second on it would be a good thing for the paper & a great thing for myself. Under almost any management but this matters

---

²²Ibid.
²³L.Q. Washington to R.M.T. Hunter, February 20, 1871, in Papers of Hunter, Hunter-Garnett Family Papers (MSS 38-45), Special Collections Department, University of Virginia Library, Reel 10.
²⁴Ibid.

would go right. But they have the paper & I am forced to other paths.[25]

Clearly L.Q. was dissatisfied with his occupational prospects. Without any respect, L.Q.'s working relationship with Barret and Harvey was untenable, and he sought any change in his fortunes. He looked to quit the *Patriot*.

Those fortunes were not quick to change. In late May 1871 L.Q. made another inquiry for the publication of Hunter's work. Once again he faced disappointment. He corresponded with journalist friend in New York, hoping to place portions of Hunter's work in the *World*; however, the anti-Southern sentiment at the time was evident. While there was caution in content, L.Q. drew his conclusion based on past experiences. L.Q. reported regretfully, "The *World* has no room (I was told) for elaborate reviews; & besides I think that it is not difficult to detect a dread of Southern ideas."[26]

L.Q. was affected by the lack of a general amnesty for the South, a personal goal since the early days of Reconstruction. He felt that the Grant Administration ignored the needs of former Southern soldiers disabled by war. He took small solace in the divided ranks of the Republicans in the Capitol. He believed even Northern citizens would tire of the harsh reactionary nature of the radical element.[27]

---

[25]Ibid.
[26]L.Q. Washington to R.M.T. Hunter, May 31, 1871, in Papers of Hunter, Hunter-Garnett Family Papers (MSS 38-45), Special Collections Department, University of Virginia Library, Reel 10.
[27]Ibid.

The rejection of southern views within the New York Democratic press signaled sectional splits elsewhere. In the state of Virginia, alliances were stalling. The Conservative alliance with Governor Gilbert Walker was cooling. Virginians resented continued Northern influence in securing lucrative government positions. L.Q. called the Governor's practice of distributing positions as "jobbery." Although he stayed clear of a shifting political situation in Richmond, doing little except corresponding with politically active friends, the convention in August saw what L.Q. called the groundwork for the "redemption" of the state.[28]

While Virginia politics embraced more Southern issues, L.Q. continued to report on the forthcoming 1872 candidate possibilities. An 1872 analysis of the political field shows L.Q.'s familiarity with the possible candidates.

> If we make no mistake in platform or candidate, I feel confident of victory. As to the latter, I feel much doubt. I should prefer Judge Thurman if I thought or rather felt sure he could carry Ohio or Penna He is the fittest man talked of & just like one of our people. Bryant--the young man is a noble fellow, but not in the race--I sometimes think it is best to run [Winfield S.] Hancock but there are grave objections to running a professional soldier. It is said Penna will ask Hancock's nomination & if so the Convention will be very apt to put him up. [Thomas] Hendricks has much in his

---

[28]L.Q. Washington to R.M.T. Hunter, July 25, 1871, Papers of Hunter, Hunter-Garnett Family Papers (MSS 38-45), Special Collections Department, University of Virginia Library, Reel 10; From the *Virginia Conservatives* by Jack P. Maddex, Jr., 101-102. Used by permission.

> favor & is popular. I am opposed to taking up any
> Republican unless perhaps Chase & even there I
> hesitate.[29]

This early analysis foreshadowed several things that indeed happened. Many good potential candidates canceled each other, resulting in the eventual nomination of a Republican to the ticket. L.Q. felt this shorted the Democratic Party. Equally distressing to him was the going-ons of the former Confederate cabinet. L.Q. lashed out at their activities.

> By the way, Stephens has taking to editing. Has there ever [been]such a vain, restless man? [Robert] Toombs has suffered himself to be "interviewed" & made foolish talk to be printed North...Davis plays the devil with his speeches. I think the comments of the Southern press have shut Davis up. <u>Nons verrons</u> as Mr. [Thomas]Ritchie would say.[30]

Despite all the fanfare surrounding the election, the second half of 1871 was hard for L.Q. Towards the end of August he came down with a severe cough. He feared tuberculosis and resolved to cure it with several vacations. He spent part of the autumn at White Sulphur Springs, followed by a return visit to

---

[29]L.Q. Washington to R.M.T. Hunter, July 25, 1871, Papers of Hunter, Hunter-Garnett Family Papers (MSS 38-45), Special Collections Department, University of Virginia Library, Reel 10.
[30]Ibid. Thomas Ritchie (1778-1854) was the longtime editor of the *Richmond Enquirer* and active participant in early Virginia politics. His paper was the centerpiece of the so-called Richmond Junto, which held political power in the state for some years.

Richmond. There he visited James Seddon and learned more of Virginia politics. Although his own health improved by Christmas, his family was shaken by the death of Washington's mother. Buried beside her husband in Washington's Congressional Cemetery, Sally Johnson Washington lived eighteen years longer than her husband.[31]

Some measure of satisfaction must been felt by L.Q. in late 1871 when hearing that his former employers, Barret and Harvey, experienced problems with the *Patriot*. The paper, weighed heavily under the rumors that it was led by New York Tammany Boss William Tweed, floundered. Harvey resigned as editor in September 1871, pleading poor health. Barret suddenly departed from the paper in late November. Shortly after, public notice of Boss Tweed's interest in the *Patriot* forced owner William Corcoran to buy out any Tammany investment and hire reputable newsmen. L.Q. hoped for some opportunity, but again was to be disappointed due to his southern ties.[32]

> Our paper here, the *Patriot*, was practically controlled by Harvey & Barret until lately. They used it for

---

[31] L.Q. Washington to R.M.T. Hunter, December 14, 1871, Papers of Hunter, Hunter-Garnett Family Papers (MSS 38-45), Special Collections Department, University of Virginia Library, Reel 10; Sally Johnson Washington, Cemetery Record Book, Congressional Cemetery, Washington, D.C.

[32] Whyte, *Uncivil War*, 98; Ibid., 122; Ibid., 126; L.Q. Washington to R.M.T. Hunter, December 14, 1871, Papers of Hunter, Hunter-Garnett Family Papers (MSS 38-45), Special Collections, University of Virginia Library, Reel 10.

personal ends & made it <u>so openly</u> <u>corrupt</u> that at last there was a movement by the stockholders headed by Corcoran to expel them. This was successful & the paper is reformed. They have nothing to do with it. I was absent when this was done. In looking about for an editor they spoke of me, but this [crossed out] it was mentioned that I had held office at Richmond with Benjamin, and this settled the matter.[33]

L.Q. was bitter at his continuing inability to duplicate success from the post-Civil War days at the *National Intelligencer*. He contributed to the reformed *Patriot*, despite his quip to Hunter that "Trustees have offered me compensation which I consider mean & unjust, & will not accept."[34] He continued his work as telegraphic correspondent for the *Louisville Ledger* and for the *London Telegraph* unabated. Despite setbacks at the *Patriot*, L.Q. hoped for assistance in the publishing industry from Democratic Senators.[35]

However, the *Patriot* faced more trouble. In March both Barret and Harvey were publicly questioned about their ties to Tweed. Further public exposure on the issue gave the paper little chance of survival. The Democratic paper depended on the upcoming 1872 Presidential election to rid itself of continuing rumors of Tammany domination.[36]

---

[33] L.Q. Washington to R.M.T. Hunter, December 14, 1871, Papers of Hunter, Hunter-Garnett Family Papers (MSS 38-45), Special Collections, University of Virginia Library, Reel 10.
[34] Ibid.
[35] Ibid.
[36] Whyte, *Uncivil War*, 132-133.

L.Q. missed much of this activity, as he again journeyed south to improve his health. Leaving the city on January 20, 1872, he stayed three days in Richmond before traveling to Charleston and the St. John's River in Florida. He stayed at Green Cove Springs for much of the next two months, touring the historic town of St. Augustine on the coast. He then returned northward.[37]

> About the 5th Mch I went to Savannah, & stayed there four days. I saw Gnl [Alexander] Lawton our old Qr Mr Genl. He is prospering & the City is prosperous. There are a number of Virginians there. I then passed two weeks at Charleston. Saw much of Trenholm & Memminger both of whom were very kind & hospitable...I then went up to visit Genl Chesnut & lady & stayed five or six days there. They are both well but he is crippled by debts & gloomy-- ...I stopped two days in Columbia & saw Barnwell.. He is well but shows age. He has nothing left but but his salary as President of the S.C. University. I left S.C. on 2d Apl & stopped at Rd near a week. I saw Seddon who is not very well or cheerful either.[38]

Now having regained his health, L.Q. considered moving to retain it. He wrote of moving to California or Western Texas.

The idea of moving was put off in the winter of 1872, as L.Q. covered the upcoming federal elections. The electoral process began with a special convention of the liberal wing of the

---

[37]L.Q. Washington to R.M.T. Hunter, April 12, 1872, Papers of Hunter, Hunter-Garnett Family Papers (MSS 38-45), Special Collections Department, University of Virginia Library, Reel 10.
[38]Ibid.

Republican Party at Cincinnati, Ohio at the beginning of May.[39] L.Q. advocated steering the convention towards moderation by flexibility. This was policy he advocated to spare the South more military-style occupation. He called the Cincinnati delegation an "imposing" one, but believed Grant could be ousted by the right candidate. He mentioned B. Gratz Brown of Missouri and David Davis of Illinois as possibilities. Nonetheless, he was uncertain if the delegates followed his ideas.[40]

> As to politics, I have been back too short a time to speak positively of public sentiment, but I think the Dems will support the nominees at Cincinnati. I see no other way to beat Grant & I am prepared to sacrifice everything else for the time to get a man in the chair who is not our implacable enemy.[41]

The results of the Cincinnati Convention surprised many. On the first ballot, Charles Francis Adams, the son of John Quincy Adams, had a firm lead. Then newspaper editor Horace Greeley of New York had a strong showing. On the sixth ballot, Greeley emerged the winner. The South, and L.Q. Washington, watched

---

[39]Ibid; James Parton, *The Life of Horace Greeley, Editor of "The New-York Tribune," From his Birth to the Present Time.* (Boston, MA: James R. Osgood and Company, 1872), 539. The Liberal Republicans by this time split from many others in the radical wing of party. They held their own convention at Cincinnati.
[40]Ibid.
[41]L.Q. Washington to R.M.T. Hunter, April 12, 1872, Papers of Hunter, Hunter-Garnett Family Papers (MSS 38-45), Special Collections, University of Virginia Library, Reel 10.

with interest to determine the benefits to the region.⁴²

L.Q. felt that an alliance with the Liberal Republicans was necessary to the continued survival of the South. He saw a split from the non-compromise Democrats as "formidable," and a source of much influence in the way of votes. He suggested this was a way to "...develope our allies & be able to blot out all the vindictive legislation. This is <u>one</u> combination & it promises, nay <u>ensures great things</u>, more than I have space to develope."⁴³ Despite his strong feelings, L.Q. knew Northern Democrats were needed to achieve any alliance. The Northern Democrats preferred one in their own party instead of Republican Greeley. However, L.Q. hoped a fusion ticket between liberal Republicans and Democrats could be formed to defeat Grant.⁴⁴

> You see what this comes to. I am for taking the Greely ticket & I believe the [crossed] firmly that if elected the South will be the favorites of his admr...You remember that our movement in 1868 & 69 saved Va. from the fate of S.C. & Louisa.[Louisiana] This is only carrying out these tactics on a national scale & the South seems to be nearly a unit for Greely.⁴⁵

---

⁴²Parton, *Life of Horace Greeley*, 543-544.
⁴³L.Q. Washington to R.M.T. Hunter, May 7, 1872, in Papers of Hunter, Hunter-Garnett Family Papers (MSS 38-45), Special Collections, University of Virginia Library, Reel 10.
⁴⁴Ibid., McJimsey, *Genteel Partisan*, 159-161.
⁴⁵L.Q. Washington to R.M.T. Hunter, May 7, 1872, Papers of Hunter, Hunter-Garnett Family Papers (MSS 38-45), Special Collections, University of Virginia Library, Reel 10.

L.Q. spent almost three pages of a letter lobbying Hunter towards the possibility of a fusion ticket between Democrats and Liberal Republicans. He urged support of the Greeley nomination. The letter was an example of L.Q.'s realistic approach to the nomination process using analytical skill and lobbying ability. He used his successful 1868 Virginia political tactics as a model for the South to find a way out of Reconstruction.

Although his political skills were solid, L.Q. was depressed over his personal situation. He remained ill during much of the spring and needed to have doctors check his lungs. From his sickbed, L.Q. observed more occupational changes at the *Patriot*. He had a distaste for the new editor Harvey procured for the paper when he exited: Richard Merrick of the *Philadelphia North American*. L.Q. claimed he was a "renegade Southerner" and used "libel" on the South.[46]

By June L.Q.'s health improved, but his occupational prospects remained bleak. He labeled the summer "the dull season for my business." He lost his engagements with the several newspapers because of his nine-month illness. L.Q. attended the Richmond Convention on June 27th and stayed at the famous Exchange Hotel, dining with John S. Barbour at a Sunday dinner and discussing state politics.[47]

---

[46]Ibid.

[47]L.Q. Washington to R.M.T. Hunter, June 18, 1872, Papers of Hunter, Hunter-Garnett Family Papers (MSS 38-45), Special Collections, University of Virginia Library.

L.Q. again stated his support for Greeley in a letter to Hunter in June. His intention was to receive a general amnesty for the South. The Democratic Convention met at Baltimore. Much to L.Q.'s delight, it favored a fusion ticket with the Liberal Republicans. Like many others, L.Q. tired of sectionalism, and wanted relief from postwar restraints on freedom.[48]

Baltimore rallied high hopes when Greeley was nominated by the Democrats as their candidate. Fusion candidacy was possible. Even more interestingly, the Democrats agreed on a platform that was essentially Greeley's: sound money, amnesty, and reform. L.Q. was fully committed and hoped that Greeley votes would appear in Richmond in early July. The prospects of Greeley's election looked promising, but state railroad interests opposed his financial reform plans. The railroad magnates spent money freely in the South and elsewhere in support of Grant. Old fashioned lobbying was no competition for cold hard cash. L.Q. was appalled over the tactics used to sway votes.[49]

> Our leaders were greatly deceived in Penna. and Ohio..In the first state I suppose there were polled

---

[48]Ibid.
[49]William Harlan Hale, *Horace Greeley-Voice of the People* (New York: Harper & Brothers, 1950), 338; L.Q. Washington to R.M.T. Hunter, July 5, 1872, Papers of Hunter, Hunter-Garnett Family Papers (MSS 38-45), Special Collections Department, University of Virginia Library, Reel 11; Hale, *Greeley*, 345; L.Q. Washington to R.M.T. Hunter, October 10, 1872, in Papers of Hunter, Hunter-Garnett Family Papers (MSS 38-45), Special Collections, University of Virginia Library, Reel 11.

> 15000 fraudulent votes & the use of an enormous campaign fund enabled our opponents to buy up in Penn: a great many Democrats-ward & district politicians, local leaders & Cameron has engineered this fraud & purchase...I fear there will be no change of policy.[50]

L.Q.'s hope for Southern amnesty turned bleak under the circumstances. He compared it to "four more years of the bayonet,-less reconstruction perhaps, but quite as much of the system of repression, bloody assizes &c."[51] Hunter asked L.Q. if he expected an office from Greeley should he be elected; L.Q. replied he did not ask for any position. In October 1872, he was employed as correspondent for three papers at a modest salary: The *Louisville Courier-Journal*, *Cincinnati Enquirer*, and *St. Louis Times*. He toyed with the idea of work with the Texas Pacific Railroad, but was reluctant to leave Washington.[52]

L.Q. engrossed himself in political activities and continued to work with Hunter on his publishing quest. The prospects improved somewhat. In the early days of 1873, L.Q. wrote Lewis Harvie that Hunter wrote about a hundred pages, but lacked the funds for additional reference material. Opportunity came when

---

[50] L.Q. Washington to R.M.T. Hunter, October 10, 1872, Papers of Hunter, Hunter-Garnett Family Papers (MSS 38-45), Special Collections, University of Virginia Library, Reel 11. Simon Cameron was a Pennsylvania politician who served as Abraham Lincoln's first Secretary of War. He was caught in a contracting scandal and left the administration in late 1861.
[51] Ibid.
[52] Ibid.

a friend suggested L.Q. work on claims cases before Congress to supplement his correspondent's work.[53]

In January 1873, L.Q. immersed himself in the duel occupations of newspaper and war claims work. In assisting the arrangement of claims through Congress, there was a little pay and the hope for Hunter's financial relief. Using his contacts in Washington, he arranged an application for the relief of disabilities created by the Fourteenth Amendment through Congress. A relief was the sole option for Hunter's occupational welfare. L.Q. consulted several politicians, and his efforts in garnering support was the catalyst for a bill sent through the House of Representatives. When the bill "vanished" in the Senate, L.Q. quickly asked Hunter for a duplicate request of the stated language, which he felt caused Hunter's claim to be tabled. Although there was opposition by West Virginia Senator Boreman, he was convinced to not oppose the measure by going "in the cloak room when the matter came up."[54]

---

[53]L.Q. Washington to R.M.T. Hunter, November 9, 1872, in Papers of Hunter, Hunter-Garnett Family Papers (MSS 38-45), Special Collections, University of Virginia Library, Reel 11; L.Q. Washington to Lewis Harvie, January 18, 1873, Harvie Family Papers, Virginia Historical Society.

[54]L.Q. Washington to R.M.T. Hunter, January 24, 1873, in Papers of Hunter, Hunter-Garnett Family Papers (MSS 38-45), Special Collections, University of Virginia Library, Reel 11; L.Q. Washington to R.M.T. Hunter, February 4, 1873, Papers of Hunter, Hunter-Garnett Family Papers (MSS 38-45), Special Collections, University of Virginia Library, Reel 11; L.Q. Washington to R.M.T. Hunter, February 13, 1873, Papers of Hunter,

> At any rate the Bill is all--so says McDonald the old clerk who manages the Senate business & returns a cordial recollection of you. He desires his remembrances to you. I shall hope now to see you in public life again either in Congress--or as Governor in Walker's place--We need persons as yourself in Congress.[55]

It was a time of mixed fortunes. L.Q. telegraphed Hunter that his application for relief was accepted on March 4, 1873. The following month found him in Richmond for the first speeches in the Governor's race. Governor Walker's term was outgoing, and political possibilities existed for Hunter and other former Confederates. In evaluating his mentor's possibility of winning some public office, L.Q. was alarmed by Hunter's financial situation, which he discovered through a mutual friend. Hunter's financial standing deteriorated in April due to his failure to file a judgment for the claim. L.Q. appealed to Lewis Harvie on behalf of friends to loan Hunter enough money to avoid possible foreclosure on his home.[56]

Hunter-Garnett Family Papers (MSS 38-45), Special Collections, University of Virginia Library, Reel 11; L.Q. Washington to R.M.T. Hunter, March 5, 1873, Papers of Hunter, Hunter-Garnett Family Papers (MSS 38-45), Special Collections, University of Virginia, Reel 11.
[55]L.Q. Washington to R.M.T. Hunter, March 5, 1873, Papers of Hunter, Hunter-Garnett Family Papers (MSS 38-45), Special Collections, University of Virginia, Reel 11.
[56]Telegraph, L.Q. Washington to R.M.T. Hunter, March 4, 1873, Papers of Hunter, Hunter-Garnett Papers (MSS 38-45), Special Collections, University of Virginia Library, Reel 11; From the

Editorial Wars, Greenbacks, and Redemption

Despite Hunter's financial difficulty, L.Q. still pushed for his political fortunes. Frank Ruffin wrote L.Q. that a movement was afoot to make Hunter Governor of Virginia. L.Q. was against the idea, and preferred another position closer to his own contacts in Washington. He reminded Hunter that the Governor's office pressed him financially. He warned there were a number of possible candidates. Former Confederate General James Lawson Kemper and Robert E. Withers were the popular leaders for the post in the spring of 1873. Kemper had an advantage with political support from former Confederate General William Mahone. Knowing these strong political connections, L.Q. advised his friend toward an office he could win easily and with less cost. In June, Hunter decided against running for Virginia Governor.[57]

> I note all you say about the Governorship & think you have answered your correspondents rightly & taken the right course. I hope you will <u>not</u> be nominated; for I cannot see that it will do you any good & I feel perfectly sure that you can go to the

---

Virginia Conservatives by Jack P. Maddex, Jr., 102-104. Used by permission; L.Q. Washington to Lewis E. Harvie, May 15, 1873, Harvie Papers, Virginia Historical Society.
[57]L.Q. Washington to R.M.T. Hunter, May 26, 1873, Papers of Hunter, Hunter-Garnett Papers (MSS 38-45), Special Collections, University of Virginia Library, Reel 11; From the *Virginia Conservatives* by Jack P. Maddex, Jr., 106. Used by Permission; L.Q. Washington to R.M.T. Hunter, June 8, 1873, Papers of Hunter, Hunter-Garnett Papers (MSS 38-45), Special Collections, University of Virginia Library, Reel 11.

Senate or House as you may prefer. The competition for the Senate cannot be much.[58]

As the process of Hunter's political rehabilitation began, L.Q.'s health improved. He joked to Hunter that he needed "ham head, greens, onions & c."[59] He sent Thomas Wynne fragments of Indian pottery from the St. John's River in Florida. He visited Lewis Harvie, James Seddon, and others in Richmond while reporting the pre-convention campaigning. For a month, L.Q. traveled to western Virginia on an independent mission for the James River & Kanawha Canal. On his return, he stopped at Richmond once again. He visited with Harvie, William Old, Gordon, and Ruffin. By mid-September, L.Q. returned to his office in the rear of Willard's Hotel.[60]

L.Q. went to work on the question of Virginia's political future. In August, the Conservative Party held their convention. As expected, Mahone's presence and his support for candidate Kemper was vital in the convention. In the general election, Kemper faced Republican Robert W. Hughes, a newspaper

---

[58]L.Q. Washington to R.M.T. Hunter, June 8, 1873, Papers of Hunter, Hunter-Garnett Papers (MSS 38-45), Special Collections, University of Virginia Library, Reel 11.
[59]Ibid.
[60]Ibid; L.Q. Washington to R.M.T. Hunter, September 16, 1873, Papers of Hunter, Hunter-Garnett Papers (MSS 38-45), Special Collections, University of Virginia Library, Reel 11; L.Q. Washington to R.M.T. Hunter, September 25, 1873, Papers of Hunter, Hunter-Garnett Papers (MSS 38-45), Special Collections, University of Virginia Library, Reel 11.

Editorial Wars, Greenbacks, and Redemption

editor. With the assistance from Mahone, Kemper won handily.[61]

As the Governor's race unfolded in Virginia, Hunter looked toward a Senatorial bid. L.Q. forged ahead with his conceived campaign, and was pleasantly surprised by Hunter's arrangements for several speaking engagements. L.Q. wanted a more extensive speaking tour, comprising Alexandria as well as Winchester and other points. He strongly advised talk of "western issues" such as free trade and governmental reforms. Unlike his standing in 1860, L.Q. acted solely in an advisory capacity. He pointed out that Montgomery Blair could help in Winchester, and he would assist Hunter's candidacy in Washington, D.C. He also arranged for regional newspapers to be sent to Hunter during the campaign to inform him of the latest public sentiment.[62]

In his research, L.Q. found potential pitfalls in the Hunter campaign. One weakness was the unfavorable criticism voiced by former Mississippi Senator Henry Foote. Although the Senator's criticism was over a long past Civil War account, L.Q. seriously considered its significance in Hunter's political future. The Hampton Roads Conference of 1865 was the subject of the

---

[61]From *Virginia Conservatives* by Jack P. Maddex, Jr., 107. Used by permission; Ibid., 109.

[62]L.Q. Washington to R.M.T. Hunter, September 16, 1873, Papers of Hunter, Hunter-Garnett Papers (MSS 38-45), Special Collections, University of Virginia Library, Reel 11; L.Q. Washington to R.M.T. Hunter, September 25, 1873, Papers of Hunter, Hunter-Garnett Papers (MSS 38-45), Special Collections, University of Virginia Library, Reel 11.

Editorial Wars, Greenbacks, and Redemption

discussion. Foote published an unfavorable account of Jefferson Davis and Hunter, blaming them for the failure of peace overtures in late 1864. Unlike his usual obsession with concerns of this nature, L.Q. advised Hunter that, "I do not think you ought to notice him-at least it does not now strike me so. But you ought to write out as fully as possible your recollection of the Hampton Roads business..."[63]

In early October, Hunter visited L.Q. in Washington. They went over the address planned before the Agricultural Society at Winchester, in which Hunter's actions at Hampton Roads were defended again. In the address, he insisted on speaking of one of Abraham Lincoln's ideas from the Hampton Roads Conference. At the time, Hunter claimed Lincoln proposed paying 400 million dollars as compensation for the loss of slave labor. The seasoned politician felt it set the tone for his audience to mention that the United States was currently bound by Lincoln's word. L.Q. disagreed with the idea, feeling that it would anger Northern Democrats. Although "tired of doing or saying things to please the North," he realized that Hunter was taking a great chance. He knew Hunter had thought much on the inclusion, but was unwilling to completely discount it without consulting others. Hunter forged ahead and gave the speech as planned on October

---

[63] L.Q. Washington to R.M.T. Hunter, September 25, 1873, Papers of Hunter, Hunter-Garnett Papers (MSS 38-45), Special Collections, University of Virginia Library, Reel 11.

Editorial Wars, Greenbacks, and Redemption

7, 1873.[64]

L.Q. felt the speech content meant disaster in Reconstruction Virginia. Hunter's other speeches at Staunton and Richmond were better received, and because of those he received the support of Kemper and Mahone. L.Q. involved himself more personally from this point of the campaign. He journeyed to Bowling Green, Virginia, to visit Hunter at his residence. L.Q. warned Hunter to stay away from interviews, and rather consult with friends such as William Gordon and Lewis Harvie. He pushed Hunter towards his closest confidantes. Ever conscious of public opinion on Hunter's speeches, L.Q. polled residents of Bowling Green on his way home.[65]

L.Q. had more free time during the campaign, largely due to a dispute with one of the papers he worked for. Newspapers found new sensationalism in the festering disputes between Spain and its colony, Cuba. Noting that by November 1873 the "row was nearly settled," L.Q. found newspapers starved for more controversial material.[66]

---

[64]L.Q. Washington to Lewis E. Harvie, October 7, 1873, Harvie Papers, Virginia Historical Society.
[65]L.Q. Washington to R.M.T. Hunter, November 26, 1873, Papers of Hunter, Hunter-Garnett Papers (MSS 38-45), Special Collections, University of Virginia Library, Reel 11; L.Q. Washington to R.M.T. Hunter, September 16, 1873, Papers of Hunter, Hunter-Garnett Papers (MSS 38-45), Special Collections, University of Virginia Library, Reel 11.
[66]Ibid.

> I have sent dispassionate despatches. One of my papers is for war anyhow & wanted me to send them war & sensational despatches to inflame the public mind which I have refused to do. I think it quite possible this may cost me my connection with that paper-the Cincinnati Enquirer. But you have no idea how much news is manufactured here & the common idea is that a correspondent must purvey lies & sensation for his papers...I expect a connection as correspondent for a Petersburg paper-the News which may enable me to give you a lift in the Senatorial race.[67]

L.Q. despaired over changes in the newspaper industry. The tone of his reporting was unlike anything that existed in his father's day. The political uses of a newspaper had changed. He wrote Lewis Harvie that old line journalists and late editors such as Thomas Ritchie or James H. Pleasants were unlikely to survive under the new conditions. "I am far from being a success in it," he wrote, "though I work very hard & have been studying my art--all since the war as well as before."[68]

By the end of November, L.Q. doubted Hunter's ability to win a Senatorial contest. He noted the Winchester speech was a bad risk given conservative sentiment, referring to it as "that foolish speech." The public reaction to the speech caused some to taint Hunter as a conservative. He prodded Harvie to get William Gordon more involved as Hunter's political advisor. Although

---

[67]Ibid.
[68]L.Q. Washington to Lewis E. Harvie, November 29, 1873, Harvie Papers, Virginia Historical Society.

L.Q. continued to push for support on Capitol Hill, by mid-December he admitted that his ability to garner endorsements were "very difficult." He wrote Hunter that "no Northern man or paper can afford or dare to endorse that speech."[69]

Despite the drawbacks, L.Q. tried quelling opposition from Northern Democratic newspapers. He communicated to New York politician David A. Wells and Frank Blair for support from their affiliates. It did no good. L.Q. wrote Hunter that the Winchester speech had cost him Blair's public support. The opposition to Hunter's candidacy used the speech against him.[70]

Hunter's campaign was effectively finished after the Winchester speech. However, L.Q. remained upbeat. On December 31st, 1873 he wrote that Hunter had twenty-four votes among Virginia electors. By canvassing Capitol Hill and contacts in Virginia, he estimated rival Gilbert Walker had only "12 to 15 votes." He discounted Barbour's strength, and felt Withers was really the prominent opponent. L.Q. campaigned near Richmond to repair Hunter's tarnished image. He stayed for a time at J.L. Carrington's Exchange Hotel and the nearby Ballard House. He was not certain if William Mahone, who had

---

[69]Ibid.; L.Q. Washington to Lewis E. Harvie, December 16, 1873, Harvie Family Papers, Virginia Historical Society; L.Q. Washington to R.M.T. Hunter, December 11, 1873, Papers of Hunter, Hunter-Garnett Family Papers (MSS 38-45), Special Collections, University of Virginia Library, Reel 11.

[70]L.Q. Washington to R.M.T. Hunter, December 11, 1873, Papers of Hunter, Hunter-Garnett Family Papers (MSS 38-45), Special Collections, University of Virginia Library, Reel 11.

supported Hunter in prior years, planned to back Hunter for the seat. L.Q. correctly noted that the Winchester speech blocked "invaluable" Northern Democratic support. As he rode back to Washington D.C. by train, L.Q. worked feverishly on balloting strategy.[71]

Despite L.Q.'s hard work on his campaign, Hunter's chances for nomination were not repaired. Two weeks after returning home, L.Q. again campaigned in Richmond. Withers gained strength quickly, having able supporters such as former Confederate General Jubal Early and John Warwick Daniel. Numerous other candidates for the Congressional post, such as John Goode of Bedford County, Robert Ould, and Gilbert Walker, siphoned off crucial segments of the vote. Even L.Q.'s close friend, Thomas Wynne, was obligated to vote for Walker as "he dared not vote against Walker when in nomination as it would cost him his place on the R.R. [Richmond & Petersburg Railroad]."[72] The final ballot dropped all names but Hunter, Withers, and Goode. However, Withers emerged victorious after garnering votes from a few key "old Whigs" as well as "young

---

[71]L.Q. Washington to R.M.T. Hunter, December 31, 1873, Papers of Hunter, Hunter-Garnett Family Papers (MSS 38-45), Special Collections, University of Virginia Library, Reel 11.

[72]L.Q. Washington to R.M.T. Hunter, January 14, 1874, Papers of Hunter, Hunter-Garnett Family Papers (MSS 38-45), Special Collections, University of Virginia Library, Reel 12; From *Virginia Conservatives* by Jack P. Maddex, Jr., 289. Used by permission; William Ernst, "Thomas Hicks Wynne," *Virginia Cavalcade,* Volume 27, No. 4, Spring 1978, 186.

men." L.Q. blamed a "secretly hostile" faction of old line Whigs and was clearly upset by the outcome.[73]

> I can not give you & myself any comfort. I am simply disgusted with the State. The people have changed by conquest. No Yankee State would have disgraced itself thus. I have only one consolation. I am not responsible for this infamy & ingratitude...I am worn out for lack of sleep & am heartsick.[74]

Although upset, he encouraged his friend Hunter.

> Be brave, firm, industrious & energetic. Use your pen freely even if you burn what you write afterwards. Be up & doing. The wheel of fortune may come around yet-Be ready for it...let the idiots in the Legislature see that you are not asleep or dead, or effete & a Bourbon.[75]

Hunter rebounded from his failed bid for office. Talented in finance, he was needed for his skills in that area, and immediately went to work on Virginia's currency. L.Q. was doubtful of his own ability in certain areas of finance. However, he stated his

---

[73]L.Q. Washington to R.M.T. Hunter, January 14, 1874, Papers of Hunter, Hunter-Garnett Family Papers (MSS 38-45), Special Collections, University of Virginia Library, Reel 12.
[74]Ibid.
[75]Ibid. The name Bourbon pertained to the French Royalty dynasty that ended in 1848. In this sense, a Bourbon was a term referring to old line secessionists in postwar conditions. Judging from Washington's phrasing, he was not endeared to the term.

great opposition to "greenbacks," or legal tender notes instead of metallic money. Although paper currency was used in the state, the history of trade paper during the 1830's influenced his opinion. The paper was not backed by hard money, so it became speculation. Many lost a fortune. In addition, the widespread financial reverses from the financial Panic of 1873 were fresh in many minds.[76]

> I care very little about the <u>legal tender</u> currency-except in this point. It is a lie & a fraud to <u>force</u> the Greenbacks as money when they are not redeemable in specie, & the Govt. should at once give up the law declaring these notes a <u>legal tender</u>.[77]

L.Q. offered to read and market Hunter's papers on the currency question. His contacts with the newspaper world were still valuable. L.Q. suggested that Hunter write to the *New York Herald* and the *World* as possible outlets for his views on currency. However, he feared backlash from Hunter's speech at Winchester. Despite the worries, copies of Hunter's currency statements found distribution in several papers. Although they found a secure place at the *Louisville Courier Journal*, Manton

---

[76] L.Q. Washington to R.M.T. Hunter, February 11, 1874, Papers of Hunter, Hunter-Garnett Family Papers (MSS 38-45), Special Collections, University of Virginia Library, Reel 12; From *Virginia Conservatives* by Jack P. Maddex, Jr., 265. Used by permission.

[77] L.Q. Washington to R.M.T. Hunter, February 11, 1874. Papers of Hunter, Hunter-Garnett Family Papers (MSS 38-45), Special Collections, University of Virginia Library, Reel 12.

Marble's *World* would only promise publication when space became available.[78]

L.Q.'s time as a simultaneous political advisor and newspaper man was a serious downturn in his career. He served as a connection for Hunter between Washington D.C. and Richmond, but L.Q. grew tired of regional politics. It was a shadow reprise of his role in 1860, but 1874 marked the last time L.Q. Washington personally immersed himself in the thick of campaigning. Although enamored with the political process, he loathed its demons. Almost fifty years old, he was again a spectator with a pen.

---

[78]Ibid; L.Q. Washington to R.M.T. Hunter, February 17, 1874, Papers of Hunter, Hunter-Garnett Family Papers (MSS 38-45), Special Collections, University of Virginia Library, Reel 12; L.Q. Washington to R.M.T. Hunter, March 5, 1874, Papers of Hunter, Hunter-Garnett Family Papers (MSS 38-45), Special Collections, University of Virginia Library, Reel 12; L.Q. Washington to R.M.T. Hunter, March 15, 1874, Papers of Hunter, Hunter-Garnett Family Papers (MSS 38-45), Special Collections, University of Virginia Library, Reel 12.

"You Owe Him Nothing"

In the Spring of 1874, L.Q. was back in the comfortable old roles of newsman and friend rather than political advisor. The aftermath of the Senate race of 1873-74 caused deep ideological divisions between Republicans and Democrats. Neither used the opportunity to compromise in Virginia. L.Q. and Hunter did not fit into any of these developing political compartments. Virginia politics leaned on revised views. Many former Confederates followed conflicting courses to conform to the changes.

By February 1874, L.Q. loathed Jefferson Davis. He felt Davis unfairly attacked Hunter on war decisions. When Hunter asked for a paper on war accounts penned by Davis, L.Q. warned him not to read them, and when Davis and former Confederate General Joseph Johnston released their memoirs of the war, L.Q. advised him to stay independent of his former ally.[1]

> You owe him nothing, as he has slandered & injured you very much. Besides your furnishing him with a report would look like an alliance with them & set all his enimies upon you. My idea would be for you to write what to write independently of him--say for a Book or magazine article, or as a Contribution to the Southern Historical Society. But I would counsel you to keep what you prepare until you can turn it to some good account for yourself.[2]

Davis' work reexamined the Hampton Roads Conference.

---

[1] L.Q. Washington to R.M.T. Hunter, February 11, 1874, Papers of Hunter, Hunter-Garnett Family Papers (MSS 38-45), Special Collections, University of Virginia Library.
[2] Ibid.

"You Owe Him Nothing"

L.Q. felt Hunter needed the consultation of Judge John A. Campbell before considering an account of his own for Davis' perusal. The unfortunate result of the fatal conference was re-evaluated several times during the 1870s. L.Q. pointed out to Hunter that the conference failed due to the unwillingness of Seward and Lincoln, not the actions of the Confederate commissioners. He noted Davis was an extremist element who had opposed the peace initiative as well.[3]

L.Q. was still bitter over Hunter's senatorial defeat the previous winter. His anger stayed strong in the summer of 1874. He avoided trips to Richmond after the nomination. In explaining his absence from the state, he wrote Lewis Harvie,

> I would not like to go to Virginia <u>now</u>. My feeling of <u>loathing</u> for the tone of our people in licking Walker's feet & all for the love of the degradation & without even a seeming <u>plea</u> of necessity is so strong that I fear they would mob me as I would them if I could.[4]

Also indicative of his isolation was a marked change in his leisure plans. Instead of vacationing at the Virginia springs, L.Q. ventured north to Fire Island, New York for "some fishing & sea bathing" in August.[5] L.Q.'s strong enmity toward Virginia in the

---

[3]L.Q. Washington to R.M.T. Hunter, March 15, 1874, Papers of Hunter, Hunter-Garnett Family Papers (MSS 38-45), Special Collections, University of Virginia Library.
[4]L.Q. Washington to Lewis E. Harvie, August 12, 1874, Harvie Papers, Virginia Historical Society.
[5]Ibid.

summer of 1874 was also largely due to persistent rumors in Richmond over Hunter's drinking, first started by the opposition during the 1873 Senate races. Although he thought the opposition's campaign tactic unfair, L.Q. had urged Hunter to completely stop drinking in order to improve his image.

After August 1874 there was a decisive decline in L.Q.'s political activity and newspaper coverage in his native state. He kept busy with a few news pieces and brief occasional visits. By early 1876 L.Q. developed a second career field, working as a clerk in two Congressional Committees. Employed under the sympathetic eye of L.Q.C. Lamar, a fellow Southerner enjoying a renewed political career, his prospects improved. In short order, L.Q. argued with Representative Washington Townsend of Pennsylvania. Although it is uncertain what the subject of the disagreement was about, the *Worcester Spy*, a Massachusetts publication, called L.Q. "a protégé of L.Q.C. Lamar." In addition, *The Spy* repeated that "[Eppa] Hunton, of Virginia, a democrat, and an ex-rebel general,

> the chairman of one of these committees, will not tolerate Washington, since his ruffianly conduct to Mr. Townsend, but Lamar cleaves to him. The result for the necessity of appointing another clerk for Mr. Hunton's Committee."[6]

The article prompted Hunton to write L.Q. a letter denying the

---

[6]Newspaper clipping from *Worcester [Mass] Spy*, attached to letter, Eppa Hunton to L.Q. Washington, March 24, 1876, Littleton Dennis Quinton Washington Papers, Duke University Special Collections.

article's accuracy. Although L.Q. had already resigned the high profile position of Lamar's clerkship, Hunton explained that he planned to appoint L.Q. to his committee. Both committees used a common clerk due to L.Q.'s resignation. Hunton maintained that he held L.Q. in the "highest respect."[7]

L.Q.'s personal life fared little better. In fact losses dogged him constantly during this period. In addition to the death of his mother and brother Peter several years earlier, one of the greatest blows occurred in 1875, when he mourned the death of his close friend Thomas Wynne at the age of fifty-five. At this time L.Q.'s previously prodigious correspondence with friends and co-workers lapsed.[8]

In January 1876 L.Q. was writing for the *Courier-Journal* and arranging for the publication of an open letter by Hunter on the subject of currency. More interested in reaction, L.Q. hoped to bolster Southern views on its most progressive occupational avenues, money and transportation. He followed the career of political ally John Randolph Tucker after his election to Congress that year. When a bill for the celebration of the country's Centennial came to the floor of the House of Representatives, L.Q. reported Tucker's oratory skills in the *Richmond Enquirer*.[9]

---

[7]Hunton to Washington, March 24, 1876, Washington Papers, Duke University Special Collections.
[8]Ernst, "Thomas Hicks Wynne," *Virginia Cavalcade*, Spring 1978, 186.
[9]L.Q. Washington to R.M.T. Hunter, January 31, 1876, Papers of Hunter, Hunter-Garnett Family Papers (MSS 38-45), Special Collections, University of Virginia Library; Typescript of Report

> The other remarkable speech was by J. Randolph Tucker, of Virginia, upon the Centennial bill. This was Mr. Tucker's debut, not only in Congress, but even in a Legislative body. Mr. Tucker showed himself completely at home, and spoke with a fine voice, that easily filled the hall, and bore himself amid several interruptions as if to the manor born...The chief value of the speech is in showing to the North that the South still has sons worthy of her glorious past, ready to do duty in the public councils. In this respect I felt proud of it, but the general structure of the speech was built upon old ideas and the old grooves which existed before the war.[10]

L.Q. indicated that Tucker reflected a "states rights" perspective toward the Centennial Bill. The fact that he feared a Southern vote against the measure was further proof that L.Q. also worried about another political gaffe along the lines of Hunter's disastrous Winchester speech. Moderation was necessary when dealing with certain elements within the Republican Party. It must have been difficult to criticize an ally for what he felt was a larger goal, but it gave L.Q. credibility in his writing.[11]

L.Q. remained detached from Virginia, though he kept up with events through correspondence to friends. He started for St.

---

by L.Q. Washington, in *Richmond Enquirer*, January 20, 1876, Tucker Family Papers, Special Collections, Leyburn Library, Washington and Lee University.
[10] Typescript by L.Q. Washington, Tucker Family Papers, Special Collections, Leyburn Library, Washington and Lee University.
[11] Ibid.

"You Owe Him Nothing"

Louis in June, but studied national politics when he covered the Hayes-Tilden Presidential Election in November 1876. Democrat Samuel J. Tilden of New York had a good chance to upset Republican Rutherford B. Hayes of Ohio. He appeared to be the first strong Democratic candidate since the war. Some Virginians, such as Governor Kemper, wanted General Winfield Scott Hancock for the job because of his honest reputation. By November the political arena was rife with possibilities. The South felt uneasy about Republican tactics at the polls to stifle regional interests. The election occurred on the 7th of November. With the balloting was too close to call, a recount was required, and a special Congressional committee was selected. L.Q. was suspicious of the Republicans, and believed that they planned to "stuff the ballot box" for Hayes by declaring the deep Southern states to be for the nominee.[12]

> I fear the Senate will be thoroughly partisan. If <u>they</u> can be held up to the <u>programme</u> of the leaders then Ferry & the majority of that body will declare that Hayes has received a majority of the electoral college and is elected. Grant will see to it that he is inaugurated

---

[12] John Goode, *Recollections of a Lifetime By John Goode of Virginia* (New York & Washington: The Neale Publishing Company, 1906), 121; Robert Rivers Jones, *Conservative Virginian: The Post-War Career of Governor James Lawson Kemper,* Dissertation, University of Virginia, 1964; Goode, *Recollections,* 128-129; Personal Papers Collection, Lewis Edwin Harvie Letters (accession 25365), L.Q. Washington, Washington D.C., to My Dear Sir, 28 Nov.1876, Archives Research Service, The Library of Virginia, Richmond, Virginia.

"You Owe Him Nothing"

> & will turn over the Govt. & <u>all its power</u> to him...If the Democrats attempt to get their rights or to put Tilden in they will have the army & navy to fight... If <u>we</u> stir a finger, it is 1861 over again & we will bear all the punishment.[13]

In his pessimistic and conspiratorial view of the election, L.Q. was correct on the final result. The count was not concluded until March 2, 1877, with Hayes beating Tilden by one electoral vote. Many questioned the proceedings leading to the election of Hayes.[14]

L.Q. turned his attention from national politics back to Virginia later in the year. Governor Kemper's term ended in January 1878, and William Mahone ran for the vacancy. By July 1877 Mahone publicly supported the policy of "readjustment" of the state's debt to a lower balance. Hunter and the Conservatives opposed Mahone's movement, and were called "Funders" for their trouble. Western Virginia favored a "Funder" candidate, Frederick W.M. Holliday of Winchester. Although there was much fanfare for the "Readjusters," Holliday won. Hunter retained his position as state treasurer.[15]

The victory was short-lived for Hunter. At the end of 1878,

---

[13]Personal Papers Collection, Lewis Edwin Harvie Letters, Washington to My Dear Sir, November 28, 1876.
[14]Goode, *Recollections*, 150.
[15]Edward Younger, ed., *The Governors of Virginia 1860-1978* (Charlottesville, VA: University Press of Virginia, 1982), 86-87; Nelson Morehouse Blake, PH.D., *William Mahone of Virginia-Soldier and Political Insurgent* (Richmond: Garrett & Massie, Publishers, 1977), University Microfilms, 150.

"You Owe Him Nothing"

the "Readjusters" gained considerable strength by working in coalition with opponents. The following year they captured the legislature in the state elections. A settlement on the state debt had been reached by time of the elections in 1879. In December the "Readjusters" killed any compromise. Hunter published a letter protesting the "Readjuster" view. Since Holliday was not politically viable, Hunter was removed from his post. L.Q. watched in disgust from Washington.[16]

> I have watched the canvass in Virginia with much interest & with a degree of mortification that words cannot express. Up to the time of the election I felt no special interest in the triumph of either party & frequently defended the re-adjusters from what I deemed unjust & violent assaults. It seemed to me that the whole canvass was needlessly violent & excited & both sides much to blame...Your removal will bring great discredit on the coalition.[17]

L.Q. kept an eye on events in Virginia, but was also watchful of national offices for Hunter. In April 1880 he wrote Hunter that a suggestion was made to President Hayes concerning a possible appointment for Hunter as Commissioner of Claims with France. In early May, L.Q. reported that Hayes was committed to another

---

[16]Younger, ed., *The Governors of Virginia*, 88-89; L.Q. Washington to R.M.T. Hunter, December 6, 1879, Papers of Hunter, Hunter-Garnett Family Papers (MSS 38-45), Special Collections, University of Virginia Library.
[17]L.Q. Washington to R.M.T. Hunter, December 6, 1879, Papers of Hunter, Hunter-Garnett Family Papers (MSS 38-45), Special Collections, University of Virginia Library.

for the appointment.[18]

In the upcoming 1880 national elections, L.Q. urged friends to participate in the political process. He wrote Lewis Harvie in late April 1880 to support Stephen Field for the presidency. He asked Harvie to accept a delegate's duties at the Democratic Convention in Cincinnati. Despite L.Q.'s enthusiasm for Field, it was Winfield Scott Hancock who was nominated. Mahone's support was crucial, and he was solidly behind Hancock. However, the Republicans countered with a formidable candidate in James A. Garfield. The latter won.[19]

Despite another Republican victory in the national arena, the "Readjusters" under Mahone dominated Virginia. Mahone was elected to Congress and "Readjuster" Governor William E. Cameron was elected in 1881. Unfortunately, Hunter and the "Funders" had little impact on policy for the state. In appreciation of past victories and thoroughly disgusted with politics, L.Q. turned to Civil War nostalgia.[20]

---

[18]L.Q. Washington to R.M.T. Hunter, April 6, 1880, Papers of Hunter, Hunter-Garnett Family Papers (MSS 38-45), Special Collections, University of Virginia Library; L.Q. Washington to R.M.T. Hunter, May 3, 1880, Papers of Hunter, Hunter-Garnett Family Papers (MSS 38-45), Special Collections, University of Virginia Library.
[19]Personal Papers Collection, Lewis Edwin Harvie Letters (accession 25365), L.Q. Washington, Washington, D.C., to My Dear Friend, 28 April, 1880, Archives Research Service, The Library of Virginia, Richmond, Virginia; Blake, *William Mahone*, 184.
[20]Charles Chilton Pearson, PH.D., *The Readjuster Movement in Virginia* (Gloucester, MA: Peter Smith, 1969), 138-141.

"You Owe Him Nothing"

A spate of research efforts on the Civil War turned L.Q.'s attention from politics. Francis Lawley, a British correspondent for the *London Telegraph*, compiled source material for a biography of L.Q.'s old supervisor and former Confederate Secretary of State, Judah Benjamin. Although the writing was in progress for some years, L.Q. was eventually interviewed.[21] Benjamin was by that time a successful barrister in Europe, and removed from his old life in Richmond. L.Q. sent a letter to Lawley to assist his biographical research sometime before May 1881, and Benjamin reviewed the correspondence for its historical accuracy. It is unknown what the letter said, but the barrister joked that L.Q.'s "ideas about English public affairs are quite wide of the mark."[22]

Also "wide of the mark" was a renewed attempt for government employment. L.Q. asked *Baltimore Sun* editor A.S. Abell for his assistance in procuring the position of Secretary of the Senate in September 1881. While Abell thought the journalist "fully qualified," he refused to sign petitions or write recommendation letters for anyone. Although he obtained other clerkships in Congress, L.Q. again was forced to return to

---

[21] William Stanley Hoole, *Lawley Covers the Confederacy* (Tuscaloosa, AL: Confederate Publishing Company, Inc., 1964), 21.
[22] Typed Copy of Letter, Judah P. Benjamin to Francis Lawley, May 13, 1881, Pierce Butler Papers, Manuscripts Department, Tulane University Library. Lawley's account was never actually finished, though Hoole noted he was working on it for thirty years.

journalism.[23]

While L.Q. toiled in his correspondence, Hunter never ceased seeking new offices through his friend. L.Q. and Randolph Tucker attempted to place Hunter on a Congressional Tariff Commission in the summer of 1882. Customarily probing support on Hunter's possibilities, L.Q. approached a powerful William Mahone and asked the readjuster not to oppose Hunter. While Mahone did not oppose the commission appointment, a lack of support was evident.[24]

The failure of an appointment for Hunter foreshadowed his final years. The mill on his estate burned. The deaths of a sister and a daughter depressed him further. He subsisted as the Port Collector for Tappahannock, his home county seat, and L.Q. could do little for his friend. Hunter aged rapidly and died on July 18, 1887. It was a quiet ending for a politician who had presidential timbre before the outbreak of the Civil War.[25]

In civic affairs, L.Q. had greater luck on his own behalf. He was one of thirty-two newspaper men who dined with the Sixth

---

[23]L.Q. Washington to A.S. Abell, September 29, 1881, Littleton Quinton Dennis Washington Papers, Duke University Special Collections.
[24]L.Q. Washington to R.M.T. Hunter, February 18, 1882, Papers of Hunter, Hunter-Garnett Family Papers (MSS 38-45), Special Collections, University of Virginia Library; L.Q. Washington to R.M.T. Hunter, May 11, 1882, Papers of Hunter, Hunter-Garnett Family Papers (MSS 38-45), Special Collections, University of Virginia Library; L.Q. Washington to R.M.T. Hunter, June 18, 1882, Papers of Hunter, Hunter-Garnett Family Papers (MSS 38-45), Special Collections, University of Virginia Library.
[25]Simms, *Hunter*, 215.

"You Owe Him Nothing"

Auditor of the Treasury in Washington's trendy Welcker Hotel on January 24, 1885. Judge R.F. Crowell invited the newsmen as his guests. Visitors came from all different views and walks of life. The dinner was significant due to the submission of a constitution and proposed by-laws of an organization, called the "Clover Club" that night. L.Q. was among the signers of these papers, representing the *New Orleans Picayune*. A week later, Ben Perley Poore was elected as president of the new club. The group changed its name to the "Gridiron Club." Famous dinners were sponsored by this organization, and the group invited prominent speakers, starting late in February 1885. News gatherers and makers met at these famous meals, with exclusive speeches given. L.Q. mysteriously resigned from the club around April, among the first to do so. No extant letter detailed the reason.[26]

L.Q.'s interest in politics continued after Hunter's death. In October 1887 he wrote his friend John H. Chamberlayne, urging him to pen an article that Virginia Democrats were "in sympathy" with the national party. In doing so, L.Q. was encouraging sectional reconciliation in the Democratic Party. He followed several of the state's cases that rose to the Supreme Court, and found satisfaction in his contact with Congressman Randolph

---

[26]Ernest George Walker, *Forty-Eight Gridiron Years-A Chronicle Written from Its Records for the Use of Members of the Gridiron Club* (Washington, D.C., privately printed, 1933), 134-135; James Free, *The First 100 Years-A Casual Chronicle of the Gridiron Club* (Washington, D.C., The Gridiron Club, 1985), 143.

"You Owe Him Nothing"

Tucker and with L.Q.C. Lamar, who served as President Cleveland's Secretary of the Interior. He wrote that Lamar was "the best man of the South" in November 1887. From his advanced position, the statesman signaled hope for Conservatives.[27]

Despite Lamar's advancement, there was no doubt that changes made since the Civil War left L.Q. bitter. He felt there was little respect for old values and personalities. He remarked to Ruffin that public addresses characterized Thomas Jefferson and Andrew Jackson as less than gentlemen. To him, these new politicians smacked of "insolence." He felt there was even only a "pretence of reverence for the character of [George]Washington by the Yankees."[28]

L.Q. chose not to participate in Civil War reunions in 1888. His view of them in May 1888 had changed from his earlier interest. His later view was that they weakened Southern political initiatives. He complained to Ruffin,

---

[27]L.Q. Washington to J.H. Chamberlayne, October 13, 1887, Chamberlayne Papers, Virginia Historical Society; L.Q. Washington to Colonel F.G. Ruffin, November 17, 1887, (#640) Francis Gildart Ruffin Papers, Southern Historical Collection, Wilson Library, The University of North Carolina at Chapel Hill; L.Q. Washington to Colonel F.G. Ruffin, November 26, 1887, Ruffin Papers, University of North Carolina at Chapel Hill; Ben: Perley Poore, *Perley's Reminiscences of Sixty Years in the National Metropolis Vol II* (Philadelphia, PA: Hubbard Brothers, Publishers, 1886), 491.

[28]L.Q. Washington to Colonel F.G. Ruffin, May 15, 1888, Ruffin Papers, Southern Historical Collection, Wilson Library, University of North Carolina at Chapel Hill.

> I am tired of these <u>reunions</u> at which Southern men meet & fraternise with the scoundrels, who have oppressed & slandered them. On all these occasions the Republican Speakers take occasion to insult-the Southern Cause, to bring up the war as a topic & to reflect in our <u>leaders</u>, and by superiority in valor instead of superior in numbers & resources;-and our fellows submit to all this like whipped dogs.[29]

L.Q. took heart in the upcoming generation of Virginians entering the political arena. Randolph Tucker's son, Henry St. George Tucker, left law for politics. The younger Tucker ran for state office from western Virginia. L.Q. quipped in a letter to the young candidate, "I saw you had the disease and since you have gone in I am glad you got the nomination. I hope you will redeem the District."[30]

L.Q. followed his friend Frank Ruffin's articles and monographs with unabashed interest. Ruffin's new work on the changing role of African-Americans in the South was controversial. Like L.Q., Ruffin was concerned with the fate of Virginia during the Reconstruction Era, writing pamphlets for regional circulation. Virginia Conservatives had a difficult time accepting changes in suffrage and status. L.Q. encouraged Ruffin

---

[29]Washington to Ruffin, May 15, 1888, Ruffin Papers, Southern Historical Collection, Wilson Library, University of North Carolina at Chapel Hill.
[30]L.Q. Washington to Henry St. George Tucker, Esq., August 7, 1888, Tucker Family Papers, Special Collections, Leyburn Library, Washington and Lee University.

"You Owe Him Nothing"

in September 1888, "I have received yours of the 12th and the pamphlet on the negro question which I have read with much interest as I do all you write."[31] He was angered at the lack of invitations to Southerners at political and social events. One of the targets of his blame was a Washington Presbyterian Minister named Sunderland. L.Q. stated that the churchman was "bitter against all Southern people & all democrats" and felt "a more infamous hypocrite or fiend never prostituted the Social Calling of Christ."[32]

With politics in disarray as far as he was concerned, L.Q. traveled again, journeying to New York City in early September 1888. He visited politicians to gauge the result of the 1888 Presidential Election between incumbent Democrat Grover Cleveland and Republican challenger Benjamin Harrison. L.Q. felt "nobody could tell how it will go."[33] While in New York, L.Q. fell sick and missed much of the political wrangling in vital New York meetings. Instead he was confined to his 5th Avenue Hotel. The end result of the election was mixed in Virginia: Cleveland took the state, but Harrison won the election.[34]

---

[31]L.Q. Washington to Colonel Frank Ruffin, September 15, 1888, Ruffin Papers, Southern Historical Collection, Wilson Library, University of North Carolina at Chapel Hill.
[32]L.Q. Washington to Colonel Frank Ruffin, November 27, 1888, Ruffin Papers, Southern Historical Collection, Wilson Library, University of North Carolina at Chapel Hill.
[33]Washington to Ruffin, September 15, 1888, Ruffin Papers, Southern Historical Collection, Wilson Library, University of North Carolina at Chapel Hill.
[34] Ibid.; Moger, *Virginia: Bourbonism to Byrd*, 62.

"You Owe Him Nothing"

After the election, many looked to some guide of change within the Democratic Party. One constant presence was Tammany Hall in New York. Even after the fall of Boss Tweed, the machine was still a strong influence in the Democratic Party. L.Q.'s own distaste for Tammany never wavered since his days at the *Daily Patriot*. L.Q. confessed to Ruffin that he knew little of the Democratic machine within Tammany Hall, but he held his suspicions who the powerful players were. He named Richard Croker and Mayor Hugh Grant as "the biggest Indians of the lot."[35]

As 1889 ushered in a new Republican administration, L.Q. was no longer a man in the thick of political hand-to-hand struggles. Rather, he turned inward and accepted his shifting fortunes. Old friends passed on and the amount of L.Q.'s correspondence was getting smaller. He had to accept any role left to him.

---

[35] L.Q. Washington to Frank Ruffin, April 9, 1889, Ruffin Papers, Southern Historical Collection, Wilson Library, University of North Carolina at Chapel Hill.

Vestige of a Legacy

By April 1889, L.Q. was tired and politically obsolete. His minor complaints, such as an inflamed finger, kept him from any travel. Although this may have been a convenient excuse, age was slowing L.Q. down. He tended more to his writings and genealogy than travel. Maintaining interest in the political scenes, he was angry over ex-Confederates who broke with the Democratic Party in Virginia. He wrote frequently of his disgust-some likely resonating from Hunter's last attempt at office.[1]

> The filthy crew from the South are all here [Washington D.C.]. I see [John S.] Mosby around everywhere. Mahone is here & all that crowd. They are fighting one-another. I feel for this administration a profound loathing--for the last one contempt.[2]

Bitter with politics, he turned to his own family legacy. Mount Vernon was sold to the Ladies Preservation Society of Mount Vernon in 1859 by his distant cousin John A. Washington. L.Q. wrote little on his connection with Mount Vernon until his involvement with a separate Centennial Committee of 1889. The group was formed for the celebration of the hundred years since George Washington took office. Feeling ignored as a distant relative of the President, he found their representative election

---

[1] L.Q. Washington to Frank Ruffin, April 20, 1889, Ruffin Papers, Southern Historical Collection, Wilson Library, University of North Carolina at Chapel Hill.
[2] Ibid. John Singleton Mosby, former Confederate cavalry officer, was a member of the Republican Party.

statement contained "impudence & Cockneyism."³ He was suspicious of the Committee selections, noting Mrs. E.P.C. Lewis as "a very good Yankee woman."⁴ Upset over the lack of notable mentions with the family name, particularly those of distinction in the South, L.Q. wrote of them.

> Hardly one of them has lent any credit or distinction to the Washington connexion. For this reason, I took pains to bring out into relief the men who had reflected Credit on the family name--Prof Hy. [Henry] A. Washington, Col John M. Washington of Buena Vista, John A. Washington--of Mt Vernon, John C. Washington of N.C., Geo. A. Washington of Tennessee & his son Joseph E. Washington & others- all men of high character & force. I was obliged to omit any mention of my own special branch though two of my half brothers now deceased were second in talent to none of the connexion.⁵

After writing an article entitled "The Washington Family," which appeared on April 14, 1889, a relative questioned L.Q. over its accuracy. Lawrence Ball wrote him that he had mistaken Miss Eugenia Washington as a Great-Grandniece of the

---

³Ibid.

⁴Ibid. His statement also was of a Ms. Stevens "of Hoboken who married Muscoe Garnett & was afterwards picked up a fortune hunter."

⁵Ibid. The two half brothers Washington wrote of were Lund, Jr. and Peter G. Washington. Both were deceased. Professor Henry A. Washington (1820-1858) was distinguished in teaching law at William & Mary in Williamsburg; John A. Washington (1820-1861) was killed in West Virginia as a Confederate officer; Joseph Washington served in Cuba in the 1880s.

President's brother Samuel rather than great-granddaughter of the same. Ball complimented L.Q. that "in other respects your article is very correct and most excellent."[6] L.Q. was soon commissioned several times to serve as a member of the Board of Visitors to Mount Vernon. This service paralleled his father's genealogical work.[7]

L.Q. assisted in the genealogical studies of his numerous cousins by referencing his father's considerable material. In answering Maud Lee Davidge of Washington D.C., he wrote "I have not been able to make-out with certainty whether the 2 brothers Col. John of Wylton and Col. Bailey Washington of Stafford (your ancestor) were sprung from John, the first emigrant..."[8] He was sure that Revolutionary War Colonel William Washington was brother to Bailey, who married Fanny Wallace of Dumfries. It must have cheered Miss Davidge to know that L.Q. stated that he personally knew her grandmother and great uncle, members of the Lee family.[9]

Aside from genealogical matters, L.Q. occupied himself with more grim tasks. He wrote Ruffin to comfort him over the death

---

[6]Mr. Lawrence Ball to L.Q. Washington, April 14, 1889, Washington Family Papers, Container 2, Manuscripts Division, Library of Congress.
[7]Commission by Virginia Governor as Member of Board of Visitors to Mt. Vernon, dated March 7, 1892; Commission by Virginia Governor as Member of Board of Visitors to Mt. Vernon, dated March 6, 1893 in Washington Family Papers, Container 2, Manuscripts Division, Library of Congress.
[8]L.Q. Washington to Miss Maud Lee Davidge, Undated, Toner Collection, Library of Congress Rare Books Division.
[9]Ibid.

of his son in late May 1889. In the message to his friend, L.Q. reviewed his own life.

> It seems to me that, if I may judge by my own experiences, there is such a preponderance of misery & disappointments in this life that it is <u>necessary</u> to <u>study</u> and cultivate fortitude, as well as to moderate expectations--I have got so far along now that I <u>expect</u> misfortunes, ingratitude, treachery, and self-seeking...I fear that I am living <u>for the present</u>- a better philosophy than none perhaps.[10]

In the summer of 1889, L.Q. traveled to Europe for three months. On his return in October 1889, his right eye was "out of fix." He was forced to quit his writing to spare the additional strain on the eyes, and deeply feared it would not heal. Unable to fully admit retirement, he remained a newsman in name.[11]

With no real occupation, L.Q. spent his time on personal financial matters. He asked Ruffin to send him updates on the politics surrounding passage of the Washington & Mt. Vernon Railway Company in January 1890. The line linked many Northern Virginia communities, such as Alexandria, with Mt. Vernon. Perhaps because of his family connections, he espoused this particular railroad bill, rather than another proposal that followed a similar route. L.Q. studied the law code and kept

---

[10] L.Q. Washington to Frank Ruffin, May 31, 1889, Ruffin Papers, Southern Historical Collection, Wilson Library, University of North Carolina at Chapel Hill.
[11] Ibid.; L.Q. Washington to Frank Ruffin, October 26, 1889, Ruffin Papers, Southern Historical Collection, University of North Carolina at Chapel Hill.

Vestige of a Legacy

track of votes on the issue.[12]

L.Q.'s attentions were not confined to the transportation bill. He wrote Ruffin that President Grover Cleveland, re-elected in 1893, adamantly opposed silver coinage and gave the President's references from the 1880s as proof. L.Q. criticized Cleveland largely out of personal dislike. However, he saved his greatest disdain for the special interests that supported the president.

> ...the leaders of Tammany are, you know, venal & always ready for a deal. This would be enough to prevent our underrating his strength but he is backed by a following in New England, theWest, & I am sorry to say, the <u>foolish</u> South. Our unfortunate people are largely to blame for their own present miserable & dangerous condition. They <u>clamored</u> for Cleveland...[13]

The fear of Tammany Hall influence had permanently embittered L.Q. toward many he assisted in the past. To him, any Southerner supporting Cleveland in the Election of 1892 was treasonous. He felt Cleveland worked outside of the Southern Democratic mainstream and slighted those in it. He felt Democratic votes from the South cast for Cleveland were simply to recapture the White House. In late 1890 wrote Ruffin, "The

---

[12]L.Q. Washington to Frank Ruffin, January 19, 1890, Ruffin Papers, Southern Historical Collection, University of North Carolina at Chapel Hill; L.Q. Washington to Frank Ruffin, February 10, 1890, Ruffin Papers, Southern Historical Collection, Wilson Library, University of North Carolina at Chapel Hill.

[13]L.Q. Washington to Frank Ruffin, September 15, 1890, Ruffin Papers, Southern Historical Collection, University of North Carolina at Chapel Hill.

Southern craze for Cleveland is not half as rational or respectable as the Sioux Indian Rage about the Messiah."[14]

In the 1890s, L.Q.'s chief concern was not politics, but a memorial statue for his friend Robert M.T. Hunter in the city of Richmond. Thomas Wright of Tappahannock wrote L.Q. in September 1891, asking for his attendance at a meeting held in Fredericksburg on October 1st. L.Q. was honored by the invitation and accepted. The result was greater than hoped. The Fredericksburg meeting proved to be the foundation of the R.M.T. Hunter Monument Association, a movement determined to, among other things, move Hunter's body from his Essex home to Richmond. L.Q. presided over the meeting. Many men were distinguished members of the committee appointed to work with the Virginia General Assembly. Among the members of the committee was former Virginia Governor Fitzhugh Lee, Major Conrad Holmes of Winchester, Frank Ruffin, and former Confederate General Eppa Hunton.[15]

The battle for the monument moved on to Richmond. In December, Joseph R. Anderson was elected chairman. After a

---

[14] L.Q. Washington to Frank Ruffin, November 26, 1890, Ruffin Papers, Southern Historical Collection, Wilson Library, University of North Carolina at Chapel Hill. Washington was referring to Wounded Knee, South Dakota.

[15] L.Q. Washington to Thomas R.B. Wright, September 19, 1891, Washington Family Papers, Container 2, Manuscripts Division, Library of Congress; "Hon. R.M.T. Hunter--An Address by Colonel L.Q. Washington--The Monument Movement Revived," in R.A. Brock, ed., *Southern Historical Society Papers, Volume XXV* (Richmond, VA: Southern Historical Society, 1897), 1991 Reprint by Broadfoot Publishing Company, 193-194.

charter of incorporation was drawn, the Association was formally recognized by the General Assembly on February 2, 1892. L.Q. was engaged in several major support activities for the Association, including an official memoir of Hunter to be written with Hunter's daughter Martha. The process took several years. L.Q. wrote large sections of text, including an address of Hunter's private life. He then wrote an extensive address published in the *Richmond Dispatch* in December 1897. It explained the Association's goals and a full life account of Hunter. L.Q.'s words were kind.[16]

> More than any one whom I have known in civic trusts, Mr. Hunter reminds me of the distinguished men of that revolutionary period--men strong, learned, composed, equal to any trust; who did not derive honor from office, but who dignified and ennobled the public station.[17]

There was not much time left to L.Q. After his sister Mary Washington Evans died on September 22, 1899, he worked harder. He busied himself with several more addresses. He provided lineage information of the Washington family to

---

[16] "Hon. R.M.T. Hunter," *Southern Historical Society Papers*, XXV, 194; Martha T. Hunter and L.Q. Washington, *A Memoir of Robert M.T. Hunter by Martha T. Hunter (His Daughter) With An Address On His Life (Prepared for the Hunter Memorial Association) by Col. L. Quinton Washington* (Washington, D.C.: The Neale Publishing Company, 1903), contents; "Hon. R.M.T. Hunter," *Southern Historical Society Papers, XXV*, 193-205.

[17] "Hon. R.M.T. Hunter," *Southern Historical Society Papers, XXV*, 205.

publisher William Stanard of Richmond and assembled his father's papers. In March 1900 L.Q. joined Bradley T. Johnson, John V. Wright, and J.A. Orr in addressing a Southern Historical Association symposium on the question of the absence of a Confederate Supreme Court.[18]

There was a certain vestige of a larger legacy L.Q. passed on during his final years. One author of the period noted that L.Q. was "probably the only living man who had the opportunity to know the inside motives and plans of Confederate diplomacy."[19] Benjamin was dead for almost ten years, and many people still questioned the hurried activity of the Confederacy's last days. Just as the Hampton Roads Conference haunted Hunter, many of the questions from the end of the war were left for L.Q. to answer. He must have realized the significance of the increasing thirst for knowledge, and he set about trying to answer some of the questions regarding the Confederate Government.

In September 1901, L.Q. wrote long detailed accounts of the Confederate Archives and the 1861-62 peace mission efforts in France in the *New York Independent*. Nothing was revealed about Canadian spies, the Copperheads, or their connection to Lincoln's assassination. Much was written in general terms, with

---

[18]Ruth Lincoln Kaye, *Hufty and Washington Families*, 66; L.Q. Washington to W.G. Stanard, December 8, 1897, Virginia Historical Society; "Why the Confederacy Had No Supreme Court," *Publications of the Southern History Association*, Vol. IV, No. 2, March 1900.

[19]James Morton Callahan, *Diplomatic History of the Southern Confederacy* (New York: Frederick Ungar Publishing Company, 1901), 23.

lengthy sketches of the Confederate Cabinet.[20] Historian James M. Callahan wondered if further information was attainable. He stated, "Perhaps there were some diplomatic missions, the details of which were not confided to him."[21]

It was uncertain how much L.Q. actually knew, but a clue was taken from a letter to Hunter's son in late January 1902. He made several detailed references on the Hampton Roads Conference, including pointing out a small error in testimony taken from a volume of the Southern Historical Society Papers. He admitted that he knew much regarding the Conference and objected to the accounts of Henry Watterson and Horace Lacy, stating that their "communications are worse than worthless."[22]

L.Q.'s health failed by January 1902, and he was confined to his home. Although his obituary accounts give no actual illness, it was noted that pneumonia was associated with his death. His niece recalled that L.Q. told her he would "die just as his mother had died," by choking. Relatives and associates hurriedly wrote him. In August, a cousin from New York City, William D.H. Washington, requested L.Q.'s assistance on a history of Washington D.C. after the Civil War. The New Yorker suggested that they "collaborate through the aid of a stenographer, as I

---

[20] "Confederate States State Department," *Southern Historical Society Papers, Vol XXIX*, 341-349.
[21] Callahan, *Diplomatic History*, 23.
[22] L.Q. Washington to P.S. Hunter, January 30, 1902, in Papers of Hunter, Hunter-Garnett Family Papers (MSS 38-45), Special Collections, University of Virginia Library.

know youare [sic] doubtless too weak to write yourself."[23]

L.Q. was weak, but able to write. In June, he exchanged letters with writer Thomas Nelson Page. In response to his first letter, L.Q. noted the writer's engraving was included in *Baker's Engraved Portraits of Washington*. However, the main reason for the exchange was a check Page sent him as a loan. L.Q. felt he might not live long enough to repay it. Therefore he refused the gracious offer.[24] On June 16th, Page wrote again, insisting L.Q. keep the money. L.Q. reminded Page in a second letter that "I have told you how slight my hold on life is and you will not be surprised if I fail to repay. I know you don't care for the money."[25]

Joseph Bryan wrote to L.Q. on August 28th regarding a paper read by Henry Adams in front of the American Antiquarian Society. L.Q. responded with criticisms about Adams' account of General Lee's heavy use of wartime guerila warfare. The fight against revision of history began, and he likely doubted Adam's version of events would see any revision.[26]

The last week of L.Q. Washington's life implied that he

---

[23]Obituary, "L.Q. Washington," *The Richmond Dispatch*, November 5, 1902; William D.H. Washington to L.Q. Washington, August 14, 1902, Washington Family Papers, Container 2, Manuscripts Division, Library of Congress.
[24]L.Q. Washington to Thomas Nelson Page, June 14, 1902, Thomas Nelson Page Papers, Duke University Special Collections.
[25]L.Q. Washington to Thomas Nelson Page, June 20, 1902, Page Papers, Duke University Special Collections.
[26]Joseph Bryan to L.Q. Washington, August 28, 1902, Joseph Bryan Letterbook, Virginia Historical Society.

Vestige of a Legacy

probably knew much more than he was telling. He realized his illness was serious, and burned large portions of his papers with only hours to live. Judah Benjamin burned much of his correspondence as well. With the burning of L.Q.'s papers, likely including his correspondence from Hunter, much was left unanswered. Some of the genealogical papers, including those of his father, were not burned.[27]

The end came on November 4, 1902. As he predicted to his niece, L.Q. went into a choking fit and died shortly after. A Washington reporter noted in the *New York Times* that the old newsman had "lived here all his life, with the exception of the period of the Civil War, when he held prominent positions in the Confederate service at Richmond."[28] On November 6th, L.Q.'s funeral was held at Trinity Church on corner of 3rd and C Streets in Northwest Washington. The interment was at Congressional Cemetery, next to his parents.[29]

Ironically, L.Q.'s final accomplishment came in 1903, when his co-authored book with Martha Hunter appeared in print. Like

---

[27] Obituary, "Col. L.Q. Washington.," *New York Times*, November 5, 1902; Obituary, "L.Q. Washington," *Richmond Dispatch*, November 5, 1902; Bearden to Anderson, March 12, 1957, Bearden Papers, Georgetown University Special Collections. The genealogical material was donated to the Library of Congress.

[28] "L.Q. Washington," *Richmond Dispatch*, November 5, 1902; Obituary, "Col. L.Q. Washington." *New York Times*, November 5, 1902.

[29] Ibid.; Obituary, "L.Q. Washington," *Richmond Dispatch*, November 5, 1902; Obituary, *The Evening Star*, November 5, 1902, microfilmed by UMI; Congressional Cemetery Logs, Congressional Cemetery.

Vestige of a Legacy

much in his life, it came at a time when little could be appreciated. For all his love of political life, he had come to disdain it; it was inevitable that he would be all but forgotten.[30]

---

[30]Hunter and Washington, *A Memoir*, title page.

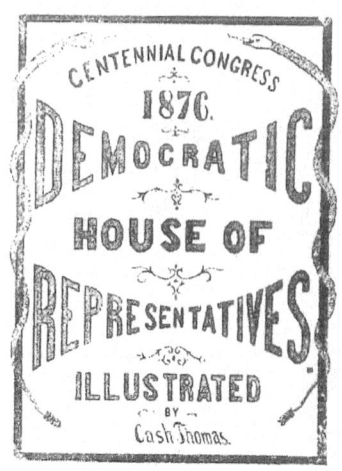 

L.Q. Washington, 1888, taken from Harper's Weekly. Top left & right, Cash Thomas poking fun at the parties in Washington regarding the Democratic Redemption. *(All Courtesy of the Library of Congress)*

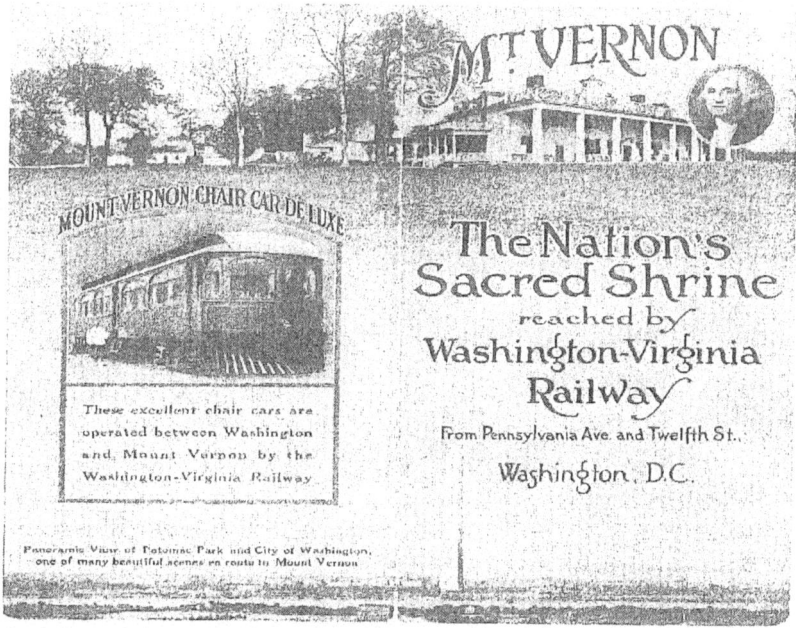

Portraits: L.Q.'s siblings Mary Washington Evans, *(Courtesy of Georgetown University)* & Peter G. Washington, *(Courtesy of The National Archives).* Above: Mt. Vernon via the Washington–Virginia Railway

George Washington's Relation to L.Q. Washington
Chart I

Rev. Lawrence Washington
(ca. 1602-1653)
m.
Amphyllis Twigden
(ca. 1602-ca. 1654)

Col. John Washington ──── *Lawrence Washington*
(ca. 1634-ca. 1677)   (1635-1677)
m.   m.
Ann Pope   Joyce Fleming
(d. 1685)   (d. ca. 1668)
| |

Maj. Lawrence Washington   *John Washington*
(1659-ca. 1697)   (b. 1671)
m.   m.
Mildred Warner   Mary Townsend
(d. 1728)   (ca. 1671-1701)
| |

Augustine Washington   *Townsend Washington*
(1694-1743) m.   (1705-ca. 1743) m.
Mary Ball   Elizabeth Lund
(ca. 1708-1789)   (d. 1778)
| |

George Washington   *Robert Washington*
(1732-1799) m.   (1729-1800) m.
Martha Custis   Alice Strother
                                                   (1731-1803)
                                                   |

                                                   Lund Washington
                                                   (1767-1853) m.
                                                   Sally Johnson
                                                   (1797-1871)
                                                   |

                                                   Littleton Dennis Quinton
                                                   Washington (1825-1902)

Lund Washington and his Children
Chart II

Lund Washington
(1767-1853)

Susannah Grayson	Sally Johnson
(1768-1822)	(1797-1871)
Peter G. Washington	Littleton Q. Washington
(d. 1872)	(1825-1902)
William Washington	Mary Mason Washington
Lund Washington	(1827-1899)
(1794-1849)	m.
Susan Washington	Dr. Warwick Evans
(1795-1829)	Emory Peyton Washington
Edward S. Lewis	(1824)
Sally Travers Hay Washington	Susan Q. Washington
(b. 1812)	(1830)
m.	Esther Matilda Washington
Socrates Maupin	(1834)
(1808-1871)	George Johnson Washington
	(1836)

First chart excludes most siblings and other marriages.
Second chart exclude descendants of marriages.

Table sources compiled from Washington Family Papers, Library of Congress; Ruth Lincoln Kaye, *Hufty and Washington Families;* and information drawn from Hugh Brogan and Charles Mosley, *American Presidential Families* (New York: Macmillan Publishing Company, copyright by Morris Genealogical Books S.A., 1993).

Bibliography

Primary Manuscripts

Andrew Johnson Papers. Manuscripts Division, Library of Congress.

Aylett Family Papers. Virginia Historical Society.

Bearden Papers. Georgetown University Special Collections.

Brock Collection. Reproduced by Permission of the Huntington Library, San Marino, California.

Case Files of Applications from Former Confederates for Presidential Pardons ("Amnesty Papers") 1865-67. M1003. National Archives and Records Administration.

Chamberlayne Papers. Virginia Historical Society.

Chisholm Papers. Virginia Historical Society.

Compiled Service Records of Confederate General and Staff Officers and Non Regimental Enlisted Men. M331. National Archives and Records Administration.

Congressional Cemetery. Burial Records.

Frank Gildart Ruffin Papers (#640). Southern Historical Collection, Wilson Library, University of North Carolina at Chapel Hill.

Harvie Family Papers. Virginia Historical Society.

Hunter-Garnett Papers (MSS 38-45). Special Collections Department, University of Virginia Library.

Bibliography

Joseph Bryan Letterbook. Virginia Historical Society.

Lancaster Family Papers. Virginia Historical Society.

Letters Received by the Confederate War Department. M437. National Archives and Records Administration.

Lewis Edwin Harvie Papers (Acc 25365). Personal Papers Collection. Archives Research Service. The Library of Virginia, Richmond, Virginia.

L.Q. Washington Papers. Virginia Historical Society.

L.Q. Washington to Miss Maud Lee Davidge. Undated. Toner College. Rare Books Division, Library of Congress.

L.Q. Washington to W.G. Stanard. December 8, 1897. Virginia Historical Society.

Littleton Dennis Quinton Washington Papers. Duke University Special Collections.

Papers of the Confederate State Department ("Pickett Papers"). Manuscripts Division, Library of Congress.

Papers of Peter Grayson Washington (MSS 2769). Special Collections Department, University of Virginia Library.

Papers of R.M.T. Hunter, Hunter-Garnett Family Papers (MSS 38-45). Special Collections Department, University of Virginia Library.

Papers of the Washington Family. Manuscripts Division, Library of Congress.

Bibliography

Pierce Butler Papers. Manuscripts Department, Tulane University Library.

Records of the Collector of Customs. RG 36. National Archives and Records Administration.

Ruffin Papers. Southern Historical Collection, University of North Carolina at Chapel Hill.

Thomas Nelson Page Papers. Duke University Special Collections.

Tucker Family Papers. Southern Historical Collection, Wilson Library, University of North Carolina at Chapel Hill.

Tucker Family Papers. Special Collections, Leyburn Library, Washington & Lee University.

Other Primary Sources

A Catalogue of the Officers and Students of Georgetown College, District of Columbia, For the Academic Year 1851-52. Baltimore, MD: John Murphy & Company, 1852.

Ambler, Charles Henry, ed. *Annual Report of the American Historical Association for the Year 1916, Vol. II. Correspondence of the Robert M.T. Hunter.* Washington, D.C.: American Historical Association, 1918.

House of Representatives Bill Number 280. Report No. 382. 28th Congress, 1st Session. National Archives.

Bibliography

Letter. October 31, 1877. *Southern Historical Society Papers, Volume IV July to December 1877.* Reprinted by Broadfoot Publishing Company, 1990.

"Letter of Hon. R.G.H. Kean, Chief Clerk of the Confederate War Department." *Southern Historical Society Papers, Volume I January to June 1876.* Reprinted by Broadfoot Publishing Company, 1990.

Martin, Isabella D. and Myrta Lockett Avery, eds. *A Diary from Dixie, as written by Mary Boykin Chesnut, wife of James Chesnut, Jr., United States Senator from South Carolina, 1859-1861, and afterward an Aide to Jefferson Davis and a Brigadier-General in the Confederate Army.* Peter Smith Publisher, Inc., Gloucester, MA, 1929.

Provine, Dorothy J. Draft Index to D.C. Marriage Records. Vol. 11-20. 1997. Copy at Historical Society of Washington, D.C.

New York Times.

Richmond Dispatch.

Richmond Enquirer.

Scarborough, William Kaufman, ed. *The Diary of Edmund Ruffin, Volume I-Toward Independence-October 1856-April 1861.* Copyright 1972 by the Louisiana State University Press. Reprinted by permission of the Louisiana State University Press.

Bibliography

War of the Rebellion: A Compilation of the Official Records of the Union and Confederate Armies. Washington, D.C.: Government Printing Office. Multiple Volumes.

Washington, L.Q. "Confederate States State Department. A Description of It by Colonel L.Q. Washington." *Southern Historical Society Papers, Volume XXIX 1901.* Reprinted by Broadfoot Publishing Company, 1991.

Washington, L.Q. "Hon. R.M.T. Hunter--An Address by Colonel L.Q. Washington--the Monument Movement Revived." *Southern Historical Society Papers, Volume XXV 1897.* Reprinted by Broadfoot Publishing Company, 1991.

Washington, Peter G. *Oration, delivered before the Association of the oldest inhabitants of the District of Columbia, in Washington, on the fourth of July, 1867, by the Hon. Peter G. Washington.* Washington, D.C.: J.T. Burch, 1867.

Washington Evening Star.

Younger, Edward ed. *Inside the Confederate Government-The Diary of Robert Garlick Hill Kean.* Copyright @ 1957 by Oxford University Press. New York, NY. Reprinted by permission of Oxford University Press.

Bibliography

Secondary Sources

Allmendinger, David F. Jr. *Ruffin-Family and Reform in the Old South*. New York, NY: Oxford University Press, 1990.

An Official Guide of the Confederate Government From 1861 to 1865 at Richmond-Showing the Location of the Public Buildings and Offices of the Confederate, State and City Governments, Residences of the Principal Officers, etc. n.p.: Ricketts Associates, 1981.

Andrews, J. Cutler. *The South Reports the Civil War*. Princeton, NJ. Copyright @ 1970 Princeton University Press. Reprinted of Princeton University Press.

Anon. "Descendants of Two John Washingtons." *Virginia Magazine of History and Biography, Volume XXVI 1918*.

Anon. "Historical Sketch of the Rockbridge Artillery, C.S. Army by a Member of the Famous Battery." *Southern Historical Society Papers, Volume XXIII*. Broadfoot Reprint 1991.

Auchampaugh, Philip Gerald, Ph.D. *James Buchanan and His Cabinet on the Eve of Secession*. Lancaster, PA: Privately Printed, 1926.

Blake, Nelson Morehouse. Ph.D. *William Mahone of Virginia-Soldier and Political Insurgent*. Richmond, Virginia: Garrett & Massie, Publishers, 1977.

Bowman, John S., ed. *The Civil War Day by Day*. Greenwich, CT: Dorset Press, Brompton Books, 1989.

Bibliography

Brogan, Hugh and Charles Mosley. *American Presidential Families*. New York, NY: Macmillan Publishing Company @ Morris Genealogical Books, S.A., 1993.

Bryan, Wilhelmus Bogert. *A History of the National Capital From Its Foundation Through the Period of the Adoption of the Organic Act, Vol. I 1790-1814*. New York, NY: The Macmillan Company, 1914.

Butler, Pierce. *Judah P. Benjamin*. Philadelphia, PA: George W. Jacobs & Company, 1906.

Callahan, James Morton. *Diplomatic History of the Southern Confederacy*. New York, NY: Frederick Ungar Publishing Company, 1901.

Dabney, Virginius. *Pistols and Pointed Pens-The Dueling Editors of Old Virginia*. Chapel Hill, NC: Algonquin Books of Chapel Hill, 1987.

Emery, Fred A. "Washington Newspaper Correspondents." *Records of the Columbia Historical Society of Washington, D.C. Volume 35-36*. Washington, D.C: Columbia Historical Society, 1935.

Ernst, William. *Virginia Cavalcade*. Vol. 27, No. 4. Spring 1978.

Fisher, John Eugene. *Statesman of the Lost Cause: R.M.T. Hunter and the Sectional Controversy, 1847-1887*. Ann Arbor, MI: UMI, 1968. Dissertation, University of Virginia.

Fite, Emerson David. *The Political Campaign of 1860*. New York, NY: The Macmillan Company, 1911.

Bibliography

Flaherty, Thomas H. et al, eds. *The Blockade-Runners and Raiders*. Alexandria, VA: Time-Life Books, 1983.

Free, James. *The First 100 Years-A Casual Chronicle of the Gridiron Club*. Washington, D.C.: The Gridiron Club, 1985.

Goode, John. *Recollections of a Lifetime By John Goode of Virginia*. New York, NY: The Neale Publishing Company, 1906.

Gunderson, Robert Gray. *Old Gentlemen's Convention-The Washington Peace Conference of 1861*. Madison, WI: University of Wisconsin Press, 1961.

Hagner, Hon. Alexander B. "History and Reminiscences of St. John's Church, Washington, D.C." *Records of the Columbia Historical Society of Washington D.C. Volume 12*. Washington, D.C: Columbia Historical Society, 1909.

Hale, William Harlan. *Horace Greeley-Voice of the People*. New York, NY: Harper & Brothers, 1950.

Hoole, William Stanley. *Lawley Covers the Confederacy*. Tuscaloosa, AL: Confederate Publishing Company, Inc., 1964.

Hunter, Martha T. and L.Q. Washington. *A Memoir of Robert M.T. Hunter by Martha T. Hunter (His Daughter) With an Address On His Life (Prepared for the Hunter Memorial Association) by Col. L. Quinton Washington*. Washington, D.C.: The Neale Publishing Company, 1903.

Bibliography

Jefferson County (WV) Historical Society. *The Washington Homes of Jefferson County, West Virginia*. Charleston, WV: Jefferson County Historical Society, 1988.

Johnson, Thomas Cary. *The Hon. Thomas Bocock.* Lynchburg, VA: J.P. Bell, n.d.

Jones, Robert Rivers. *Conservative Virginian: The Post-War Career of Governor James Lawson Kemper*. PhD Dissertation. University of Virginia, 1964.

Kaye, Ruth Lincoln. *Hufty and Washington Families.* Typescript. 1997.

Keene, Jesse L. *The Peace Conference of 1861*. Tuscaloosa, AL: Confederate Publishing Co., Inc., 1961.

Klement, Frank L. *The Copperheads in the Middle West.* Chicago, IL: University of Chicago Press, 1960.

Lewis, Edward A., Edward S. Lewis II, Edward McE. Lewis, and Lund Washington, comp. *Pedigrees of Lewis and Kindred Lines.* Manuscript. Missouri Historical Society of St. Louis, Missouri, 1927.

Lewis, Edward S. "Ancestry of James Monroe." *William & Mary College Quarterly. Volume 3, Series 2.* 1973.

Lincoln Herald. Vol. 51, December 1949.

Lowe, Richard. *Republicans and Reconstruction in Virginia, 1856-70*. Charlottesville, VA: University Press of Virginia. 1991.

Bibliography

Maddox, Jack P. *The Virginia Conservatives 1867-1879-A Study in Reconstruction Politics*. Copyright (c) 1970 by The University of North Carolina Press. Used by permission of the publisher.

McJimsey, George. *Genteel Partisan: Manton Marble, 1834-1917*. Ames, IA: The Iowa State Press, 1971.

Meade, Robert Douthat. *Judah P. Benjamin-Confederate Statesman*. Copyright @ 1943. Oxford University Press, New York, NY. Reprinted by permission of Oxford University Press.

Medical Society of the District of Columbia, *History of the Medical Society of the District of Columbia*. Washington, D.C.: Medical Society, 1909.

Moger, Allen W. *Virginia-Bourbonism to Byrd 1870-1925*. Charlottesville, Va: University Press, 1968.

Parton, James. *The Life of Horace Greeley, Editor of "The New-York Tribune," From his Birth to the Present Time*. Boston, MA: James R. Osgood and Company, 1872.

Pearson, Charles Chilton. Ph.D. *The Readjuster Movement in Virginia*. Gloucester, MA: Peter Smith, 1969.

Poore, Ben: Perley. *Perley's Reminiscences of Sixty Years in the National Metropolis Vol II*. Philadelphia, Pa: Hubbard Brothers, Publishers, 1886.

Pulley, Raymond H. *Old Virginia Restored-An Interpretation of the Progressive Impulse 1870-1930*. Charlotteville, VA: University Press of Virginia, 1968.

Bibliography

Robertson, Alexander F. *Alexander Hugh Holmes Stuart-A Biography*. Richmond, VA: William Byrd Press, Inc., Printers. 1925.

Shannon, J. Harry. "Rambler's Explorations Lead Him to Several Literary Circles," *The Washington Star Sunday Magazine*, February 20, 1927, Vol. 2, No. 136.

Simms, Henry Harrison. *The Life of Robert M.T. Hunter*. Richmond, VA: William Byrd Press, 1935.

Smith, William Ernest. *The Francis Preston Blair Family in Politics, Volume II*. New York, NY: Da Capo Press, 1969.

Stapleton, John F. M.D. *Upward Journey-The Story of Internal Medicine at Georgetown 1851-1981*. Washington, D.C.: Georgetown University Medical Center. 1996.

Topham, Washington. "First Railroad into Washington and Its Three Depots." *Records of the Columbia Historical Society of Washington, D.C.* Washington, D.C.: Columbia Historical Society. 1925.

Unknown. *The Harvie Family*. Richmond, VA: n.p., 1928.

Virginia Historical Society. *Publications of the Southern History Association*. Vol. IV, No. 2, 1900.

Virginia Cavalcade. Vol. 27, No. 4. Spring 1978.

Virginia Magazine of History & Biography. Vol. XXVI. 1918.

Bibliography

Walker, Ernest George. *Forty-Eight Gridiron Years-A Chronicle Written from Its Records for the Use of Members of the Gridiron Club.* Washington, D.C.: Privately Printed, 1933.

Walther, Eric H. *The Fire-Eaters.* Baton Rouge, LA: Louisiana State University Press, 1992.

Whyte, James H. *The Uncivil War-Washington During the Reconstruction 1865-1878.* New York, NY: Twayne Publishers, 1958.

Younger, Edward. ed. *The Governors of Virginia 1860-1978.* Charlottesville, VA: University Press of Virginia, 1982.

Index

Abell, A.S.	131
Adams, Charles Francis	104
Adams, Henry	147
Adams, (President) John Quincy	104
Albion	3, 4
Alexander, Robert	75
Alexandria, Virginia	4, 11-12, 113, 141
Amelia County, Virginia	2
American Antiquarian Society	147
Anderson, Joseph R.	143
Anderson, (Colonel) Robert	27
Andersonville, Georgia	69
Appleton Family	94-95
Arlington, Virginia	35
Aylett, Patrick Henry	23
Aylett, William R.	72
Ball, Lawrence	139-140
Baltimore Convention (1860)	21-22
Baltimore, Maryland	20, 22, 107
Barbour, James	90
Barbour, John Strode	90, 106, 117
Barret, James G.	91, 93, 97-98, 101-102
Battle of Chancellorsville	53
Battle of First Manassas	36-37
Battle of Gettysburg	53, 81
Battle of Second Manassas	44, 47
Battle of Sharpsburg	47-48
Beauregard, (General) P.G.T.	31
Bedford County, Virginia	118
Bee, (General) Bernard	36
Benjamin, Judah	1-2, 40-44, 47-50, 57-59, 61-63, 102, 131, 145, 148
Berkeley, Lord	4
Blackwood's Magazine	43, 49

Index

Blair
    Family   78-79
    Francis Preston   61, 67
    Francis Preston Jr. (Frank)   78, 82-84, 117
    Montgomery   83-85, 113
Bocock, Thomas Stanley   78
Bonham, (General) Milledge Luke   34-35
Booth, John Wilkes   62
Boreman, (Senator) Arthur I.   109
Boston, Massachusetts   6
"Bourbons"   119
Bowen, Thomas   9
Bowling Green, Virginia   115
Breckinridge, John C.   20-21
Bromwell, William   63
Brown, B. Gratz   104
Brown, John   18-19
Browne, William M.   40-41
Bryan, Joseph   147
Buchanan, (President) James   16, 17, 20
Buckingham County, Virginia   78
Bunch, (Consul) Robert   48
Burdick, Henry   8
Butler, (General) Benjamin   82
Calhoun, John C.   7, 10
Camp Pickens, Virginia   34-35
Campbell, John A.   61, 66, 68, 123
Campbell, Kate   66-67
Carlisle, Pennsylvania   10
Carrington, J.L.   117
Centreville, Virginia   34-35
Chalmers, John   8
Chamberlayne, John H.   133
Charleston Convention (1860)   22
Charleston, South Carolina   6, 20, 31, 51-52, 103
Charlotte, North Carolina   62-63

Index

Chase, Justice Salmon P.	82-83, 100
Chesnut, (General) James	23, 52-53, 93, 103
Chesnut, Mary Boykin	45-46, 52-53, 93, 103
Chotank Creek	4
Cincinnati Convention (1872)	103-104
Cincinnati Convention (1880)	130
City Point, Virginia	61
Clay, Clement C.	58
Clendinen, Doctor A.C.	54-55
Cleveland, (President) Grover	134, 136, 142-143
Clingman, Thomas	83
Coleman, William D.	74
Columbia, South Carolina	103
Committee of Nine	88
Congressional Cemetery	13, 101, 148
Cooke, John Esten	92
Corcoran, William W.	2, 91, 101-102
Coyle, John H.	79
Crenshaw, Louis	67
Crittenden, J.J.	28
Croker, Richard	137
Crossfield, Peggy	8
Crowell, (Judge) R.F.	133
Dade, Townsend	3
Daniel, John Moncure	38, 71
Daniel, John Warwick	118
Danville, Virginia	62-63, 74
Davidge, Maud Lee	140
Davis, David	104
Davis, (CSA President) Jefferson	26, 37-41, 53, 58-59, 61, 63, 92-93, 95, 100, 114, 122-123
Denver, (Judge)	68
Dickinson College	10
Donn, Thomas	9
Douglas, Stephen A.	20-22, 28

Index

Dry Tortugas, Florida (Fort Jefferson)	27
Dumfries, Virginia	140
Early, Jubal A.	118
Eckert, (Colonel) William	61
Edinburg(h) Quarterly	49
Elmira, New York	62
Essex County, Virginia	19, 143
Evans, (Dr.) Warwick (bro-in-law to L.Q.)	32, 89
Evans, (Colonel) Nathan	36
Evarts, William	67
Fairfax Court House, Virginia	34-36
Field, Stephen	130
Foote, (Senator) Henry	113-114
Forrest, (General) Nathan B.	83
Fort Pickens, South Carolina	27, 29-30, 36
Fort Pulaski, Georgia	65-66, 69
Fort Sumter, South Carolina	23, 27, 30-32
Fredericksburg, Virginia	143
"Funders"	128, 130
Galaxy Magazine	92
Gales, Joseph Jr.	6, 49
Garfield, (President) James A.	130
Garnett Family	70
Georgetown	8, 32
Gholson, (Judge) Thomas S.	23
Goode, John	113, 118
Gordon, (General) John B.	83
Gordon, William	112, 115-116
Grant, (Mayor) Hugh	137
Grant, (President & General) Ulysses S.	61, 81, 84-87, 96-98, 104-105, 107, 127-128
Grayson, William	4
Greeley, Horace	43, 105-108
Green Cove Springs, Florida	103
Greensboro, North Carolina	62-63

Index

Hamilton, Alexander	6
Hampton, (General) Wade	86
Hancock, (General) Winfield Scott	81, 83, 99, 127, 130
Handy, (Colonel) Leven	7
Hardeeville, South Carolina	46
Harper's Ferry, Virginia (now WV)	18-19
Harvey, James E.	91-93, 95-98, 101-102
Harvie, Lewis	2, 25, 94-95, 108, 110, 112, 115-116, 123, 130
Harvie, (Major) John Blair	53-56
Hayes, (President) Rutherford B.	127-130
Hendricks, Thomas	99-100
Holliday, Frederick W.M.	128-129
Holmes, (Major) Conrad	143
Hooe, (Colonel) R.T.	4
Hooper, J.J.	29
Hotze, Henry	43
Hubard, (Colonel) E.W.	67
Hughes, (Judge)	68
Hughes, Robert W.	112-113
Hunter, Martha	144, 148
Hunter, Robert Mercer Taliaferro	1-2, 19-23, 25-26, 38-41, 57, 61, 63, 65-70, 73, 77-78, 80-82, 84-85, 88-95, 97-98, 106-120, 122-124, 126, 128-130, 132-133, 138, 143-146, 148
Hunter, Mrs. R.M.T.	66-67
Hunton, Eppa	124-125, 143
Jackson, (President) Andrew	134
Jackson, (General) Thomas J. "Stonewall"	36
James River & Kanawha Canal	112
Jefferson, (President) Thomas	6, 134
Jefferson County, Virginia (WV)	17

Index

Johnson, (President) Andrew	65, 67-68, 74, 79, 86-87
Johnson, Bradley T.	145
Johnson, John	7
Johnson, Susanna	7
Johnson's Bay, Maryland	7
Johnston, (General) Joseph	66, 122
Kean, Robert G.H.	69-70
Keily, A.M.	73
Kemper, (General) James Lawson	35, 111-113, 115, 127-128
Kenner, Duncan	44, 60
Key West, Florida	31
King William County, Virginia	72
Lacy, Horace	146
Ladies Preservation Society Mt. Vernon	138
Lafayette Square	6
Lamar, L.Q.C.	1, 124-125, 134
Latham, Milton S.	16-17
Lawley, Francis	41n, 131
Lawton, (General) Alexander	103
Lee	
(General) Edward Gray	62
Family	76, 140
(Governor) Fitzhugh	143
George Washington Custis	76
(General) Robert E.	46, 59-60, 62, 65, 76, 147
Lewis, Mrs. E.P.C.	139
Lincoln, (President) Abraham	1, 23-25, 30, 61-62, 79, 114, 123, 145
London, Daniel	23
Lyons, James	80
Mahone, William	86, 88, 111-113, 115, 117-118, 128, 130, 132, 138

Index

Manassas, Virginia	34, 37
Marble, Manton	92, 120-121
Mason, James Murray	14, 16, 23, 25-26, 37, 43, 93
McClellan, (General) George B.	42, 45-46
McAllister, (Judge) Matthew Hall	15
McDowell, (General) Irwin	36
McWillie, (Governor) William	23
Memminger, Christopher	45, 103
Merrick, Richard	106
Mobile, Alabama	29, 70
Monroe, (President) James	4, 7
Montgomery, Alabama	25-26, 29
Moore, (General) Sydenham	19
Mosby, John Singleton	138
Mount Vernon	138-141
Napoleon, Emperor Louis (Napoleon III)	44, 47-48
New Orleans, Louisiana	42, 44, 70
Newspapers	
Baltimore Sun	131
Boston Globe	80
Cincinnati Enquirer	84, 108, 116
Daily Patriot	95, 97-98, 101-102, 106, 137
London Telegraph (Daily Telegraph)	43, 74, 84, 89, 93-94, 102, 131
London Times	43
Louisville Courier-Journal	108, 120, 125
Louisville Ledger	93, 102
Memphis Bulletin	73
National Intelligencer	6, 77, 79-80, 82, 84, 89-90, 93, 102
New Orleans Picayune	133
New York Herald	49, 80, 120
New York Independent	145
New York Times	49, 148

Index

Newspapers, Continued
- *New York Tribune* — 43
- *New York World* — 80, 89, 92, 98, 120-121
- *Petersburg Index* — 89
- *Philadelphia North American* — 106
- *Richmond Dispatch* — 144
- *Richmond Enquirer* — 73, 75, 125
- *Richmond Examiner* — 38, 71-73
- *St. Louis Times* — 108
- *Saturday Review* — 49
- *Worcester Spy* — 124

Old, William W. — 21, 112
Orr, J.A. — 145
Ould, Robert — 94, 118
Page, Thomas Nelson — 147
Panic of 1873 — 120
Pensacola, Florida — 27, 29, 31
Perkins, (Judge) — 22
Peters, (Colonel) William E. — 53-56
Petersburg, Virginia — 60, 73
Pierce, (President) Franklin — 14, 16
Pierrepont, (Governor) Francis H. — 66-67, 74
Pleasants, James H. — 116
Poe, Edgar Allen — 38
Pollard, Garland — 71-72
Poore, Ben Purley — 80, 133
Potomac River — 4
Railroads
- Baltimore & Ohio Railroad — 90
- Chesapeake & Ohio Railroad Co. — 76
- Orange & Alexandria Railroad — 90
- Richmond & Petersburg Railroad — 118
- Virginia Midland — 90
- Texas Pacific Railroad — 108
- Washington & Mt. Vernon RR Co. — 141

Index

Rhett, Robert B. Jr.	83
Richmond, Virginia	19, 24-26, 32, 34, 37-40, 42, 45-47, 50, 52-53, 56-57, 59-60, 63, 65-66, 72-73, 75, 77, 80, 85, 89, 91, 95, 99, 101-103, 106-107, 110, 112, 115, 117-118, 121, 123-124, 131, 143, 145, 148
Riggs, George W.	91
Ritchie, Thomas	100, 116
Robinson, John G.	8
Ruffin, Edmund	18-19, 23-24, 32
Ruffin, Francis Gildart	2, 91, 111-112, 134-137, 140-143
Russell, Earl John	48
Sams, (Captain) Horace H.	46-47
San Francisco, California	14-18
Sanders, George N.	48
Sanders, Lewis	59-60
Santo Domingo	31
Schofield, (General) John	81
Schurz, Carl	96
Scribner, Charles	95, 97
Seaton, William W.	6, 49, 77
Seddon, James A.	2, 50-51, 61, 63, 67, 69, 95, 100, 103, 112
Semmes, Rafael	73
Seven Days' Battles	44, 46
Seward, William H.	30, 61, 123
Seymour, Horatio	83-84, 86
Sherman, (Captain) Charles K.	51
Sherman, (General) William T.	60
Shockoe Hill	39
Slidell, John	21, 43, 47

Index

Smith, Dick	73
Southern Historical Society	122, 145-146
Snow Hill, Maryland	7-9
Speed, James	66
St. Albans, Vermont	60
St. Augustine, Florida	103
St. Louis, Missouri	126-127
St. Martin, Jules	42
Stanard, William	145
Stanton, Edwin	68
Staunton, Virginia	115
Stephens, Alexander	61, 63, 70, 93, 97, 100
Stevens, Thaddeus	74
Stevenson, J.W.	83
Stoneman, (General) George	52
Stuart, Alexander H.H.	57-58, 77-78, 86, 88
Stuart, (Reverend) William	3
Sumner, Charles	96
Sunderland, (Minister)	136
Surratt, John H.	62
Sweet Springs, Virginia (WV)	76
Tammany Hall	96, 101-102, 137, 142
Tappahanock, Virginia	132, 143
Thompson, Jacob	58-59
Tilden, Samuel J.	127-128
Toombs, Robert	26, 39, 100
Townsend, Francis	4
Townsend, Robert	3
Townsend, Washington	124
Trent Affair	42-43
Tucker, Henry St. George	135
Tucker, John Randolph	78-79, 85, 125-126, 132-135
Tweed, "Boss"	101-102, 137
Tyler, (President) John	24
Underwood Convention	76-77, 81-82, 84, 86

Index

University Publishing	95
Vallandigham, Clement	57-59
Van Lew, Elizabeth	50-51
Van Ness, (Mayor) John Peter	6
Vienna, Virginia	35
Walker, Gilbert C.	88, 99, 110, 117-118, 123
Walker, Leroy Pope	25-31
Walker, Robert	10
Wallace, Fanny	140
Wallach, (Mayor) Richard	66
Warrenton, Virginia	11
Warrenton Sulphur Springs, Virginia	11-12
Washington	
Bailey	140
Benjamin Franklin	17
Betsey (half-sister of L.Q.)	8
Emory Peyton (brother of L.Q.)	8
Esther Matilda	9
Eugenia	139-140
(President) George	1, 3-5, 7, 11, 17, 134, 138
George A.	139
George Johnson (brother of L.Q.)	9
Henry	139
(Colonel) John	4, 140
(Lt. Colonel) John A.	138-139
John C.	139
(Colonel) John M.	139
Joseph E.	139
Lawrence	4, 17
Littleton Dennis Quinton	
Birth	1, 9
and Washington Centennial	138-140
and *Richmond Examiner*	38, 72-73
as Congressional Employee	124-125

Index

Washington, Littleton Dennis Quinton Continued
- and Gridiron Club — 132-133
- at Hampton Roads Meeting — 60-61, 92-93, 113-114, 122-123, 145-146
- Death — 2, 146-148
- Education — 10
- in California — 14-18
- Pardoned — 65-66
- Lund (father of L.Q.) — 2-13
- Lund (great-uncle of L.Q.) — 3, 11
- Lund (half-brother of L.Q.) — 7, 8
- Mary Mason (sister of L.Q.) — 9, 10, 12, 32, 54, 144
- Peter Grayson (brother of L.Q.) — 7, 12, 15-16, 62-63, 67-68, 125
- Robert (grandfather of L.Q.) — 3
- Sally Johnson (mother of L.Q.) — 7-8, 12, 101, 125
- Samuel — 140
- Susan (half-sister of L.Q.) — 8
- Susan Quinton (sister of L.Q.) — 9
- Susannah Monroe Grayson — 4, 7
- (Colonel) William — 140
- William D.H. — 146-147
- William T. (half-brother of L.Q.) — 7, 10

Washington, District of Columbia — 1-2, 5-6, 12, 16-20, 23-24, 31-33, 35-36, 52, 62, 65-66, 70-71, 74, 78, 80, 82, 85, 89, 91, 93-95, 98, 108-109, 111, 113-114, 117-118, 121, 129, 133, 136, 138, 140, 148

Washington Library Company — 14
Washington Peace Conference — 24-25
Watterson, Henry — 146

Index

Wells, David A.	117
Wells, (Governor) Henry	85-86
Westminster Review	49
White Sulphur Springs, Virginia (WV)	11-12, 22-23, 71, 76, 84-85, 93, 100
Wickham, Williams C.	85
Wilmington, North Carolina	52
Wilson, Henry	96
Winchester, Virginia	113-114, 116-117, 120, 126, 143
Wise, Henry Alexander	2, 18, 20
Wise, John H.	17-18
Withers, Robert E.	111, 117-118
Wright, John V.	145
Wright, Thomas	143
Wynne, Thomas H.	71-72, 112, 125
York River	42
Yorktown, Virginia	44
Young Men's Democratic Club	15
Yancey, Robert	20, 26

ABOUT THE AUTHOR

David Scott Turk was born in Washington, D.C. on February 2, 1964. He received a Bachelor's Degree from Longwood College in 1986 and a Master's Degree in U.S. History from George Mason University in 1997. He has worked for several years in the history field within the U.S. Government. He is the author of *The Union Hole* (Heritage Books, 1994) and *The Memorialists* (Heritage Books, 1997), as well as several articles for journals such as *Virginia Cavalcade* and *West Virginia History*. He lives with his wife Janet and son Ryan in Fairfax, Virginia.

www.ingramcontent.com/pod-product-compliance
Lightning Source LLC
Chambersburg PA
CBHW070917180426
43192CB00037B/1650